®
teach
yourself

**making money in
the Second Life world**

making money in
the Second Life world

irie tsure

Launched in 1938, the **teach yourself** series grew rapidly in response to the world's wartime needs. Loved and trusted by over 50 million readers, the series has continued to respond to society's changing interests and passions and now, 70 years on, includes over 500 titles, from Arabic and Beekeeping to Yoga and Zulu. What would you like to learn?

Be where you want to be with **teach yourself**

For UK order enquiries: please contact Bookpoint Ltd, 130 Milton Park, Abingdon, Oxon OX14 4SB. Telephone: +44 (0)1235 827720. Fax: +44 (0)1235 400454. Lines are open 09.00–17.00, Monday to Saturday, with a 24-hour message answering service. Details about our titles and how to order are available at www.teachyourself.co.uk.

For USA order enquiries: please contact McGraw-Hill Customer Services, PO Box 545, Blacklick, OH 43004-0545, USA. Telephone: 1-800-722-4726. Fax: 1-614-755-5645.

For Canada order enquiries: please contact McGraw-Hill Ryerson Ltd, 300 Water St, Whitby, Ontario L1N 9B6, Canada. Telephone: 905 430 5000. Fax: 905 430 5020.

Long renowned as the authoritative source for self-guided learning – with more than 50 million copies sold worldwide – the **teach yourself** series includes over 500 titles in the fields of languages, crafts, hobbies, business, computing and education.

British Library Cataloguing in Publication Data: a catalogue record for this title is available from The British Library.

Library of Congress Catalog Card Number: on file.

First published in UK 2008 by Hodder Education, part of Hachette Livre UK, 338 Euston Road, London NW1 3BH.

First published in USA 2008 by The McGraw-Hill Companies Inc.

The **teach yourself** name is a registered trademark of Hodder Headline.

Computer hardware and software brand names mentioned in this book are protected by their respective trademarks and are acknowledged.

Notice and Disclaimer. Linden Lab and Second Life are trademarks of Linden Research, Inc. Teach Yourself Making Money in the Second Life World is not affiliated with or sponsored by Linden Research.

The publisher has used its best endeavours to ensure that the URLs for external websites referred to in this book are correct and active at the time of going to press. However, the publisher has no responsibility for the websites and can give no guarantee that a site will remain live or that the content is or will remain appropriate.

Typeset by Mac Bride, Southampton

Printed in Great Britain for Hodder Education, an Hachette Livre UK Company, 338 Euston Road, London NW1 3BH, by CPI Cox & Wyman, Reading, Berkshire RG1 8EX.

Hachette Livre UK's policy is to use papers that are natural, renewable and recyclable products and made from wood grown in sustainable forests. The logging and manufacturing processes are expected to conform to the environmental regulations of the country of origin.

Impression number 10 9 8 7 6 5 4 3 2 1

Year 2011 2010 2009 2008

contents

preface

The concept of making money from a virtual world proves an attractive proposition for very many Second Life residents. We've read the articles about the 'millionairess' Anshe Chung, you may also have visited our resort and it is not surprising therefore that residents aspire to generating real money by becoming a land-baron like Anshe or operating a successful and profitable venue such as Irie Vibes.

Income from Second Life seems so attainable. In-world businesses can be cheap to set-up and therefore profitability appears to be guaranteed. With 15,000,000 residents surely we can open any old project and it will quickly be packed and profitable? Second Life is a modern day gold-rush isn't it? Grab your land, set up your business, sit back and watch the money roll in.

I've scanned some other scribblings written with the intention of assisting budding Second Life entrepreneurs and in my assessment much of their analysis seems to be 'to learn skills but you will find that time-consuming', and/or 'you'll need to buy at least a quarter sim to get started then hire experts'. Well, the first 'insight' is the very definition of 'stating the blindingly obvious' and the second is pure absurdity on two counts:

- The notion of 'investing' several hundred or even worse several thousand real world US dollars into a Second Life enterprise is frequently not a financial possibility (it certainly wasn't for me).

- Prejudging an unknown market is a rapid route to losses (only going into business with your latest Second Life sweetheart will lead to a more certain commercial collapse).

The overwhelming majority of Second Life businesses fail, leaving the virtual landscape strewn with the skeletal remnants of its residents' grandest plans. Partnerships dissolve, money is lost, angst is riven, curses thrown, Second Life is criticized then often abandoned.

Unfortunately yet another resident has had an impractical fantasy, an expensive hobby at best, and the facts speak for themselves. From the economic statistics supplied by Linden Lab we can deduce (until July 2008) that less than two hundred Second Life residents generate an in-world income of over US$5000 a month with a further couple of thousand or so earning over US$500 a month. What should also be noted is that these figures exclude tier costs (a resident's largest overhead) and are not, therefore, an accurate reflection of residents' profits. And this is from a pool of the hundreds of thousands of residents who are attempting to 'turn a buck'! Why is it that so few residents succeed?

The answer is quite simple. Running a successful in-world business requires skills, ingenuity and/or hard work. There are seldom short-cuts. You cannot open a Second Life nightclub or retail outlet (or even write a book on the subject), fill it with predictable banality and mediocrity, invest too little time in the project and then expect the 'enterprise' to generate its own momentum. Don't look to someone else to do the hard work.

The financially successful residents of Second Life have common qualities. They work long and hard, they are committed, they are focused, they are adaptable creatures and have learned quickly from their mistakes. They have also taken risks in order to identify new opportunities.

These residents have trodden paths into the wilderness that are now clear enough for others to follow. They have laid the foundations to a virtual economy. But Second Life remains a new world and I do believe that these pioneers, breathtaking though their contributions have been, have merely sipped from the vast ocean of opportunity that lies before us all.

The Second Life marketplace is neither established nor predictable. There is no correct method of doing things, no sure-fire strategies for success and no specific sector that carries any guarantee. Identifying, testing, exploring and growing opportunities is the key right now, not inflicting your own 'it's bound to work!' thinking on other residents. It is important to be adaptable. Grow those concepts that work and abandon those that don't.

Making money in Second Life is not so difficult as long as we understand that making money is not 'spending money'. If your project burns cash then it will be a hobby and for me, business in a virtual world means meeting then exceeding your costs. If it is not important to you that the project covers its own costs then this book is not for you.

Residents may want to make money from Second Life to:

1 **Profit take,** i.e. to generate meaningful real-world income.

2 **Profit make,** i.e. to finance other in-world activities or to re-invest into growth.

Residents may alternatively wish to set up an in-world business:

1 **As social entrepreneurs,** i.e. to be involved with and contribute to the wider Second Life community.

2 **To create personal purpose** through an enterprise.

But ultimately it is neither fun nor satisfying to run a failing business so whatever our purpose, if the enterprise is not measurably self-financing then experience shows that the project will sooner or later become just another Second Life carcass.

If however, without investing anything but time and effort, you find the idea of generating (to start with) an extra few hundred dollars a month attractive, then you and I are on the same wavelength and I hope this book will prove useful.

This book will enable you, whatever your reason for reaching into Second Life's world of virtual commerce, to identify and learn the skills and strategies required to prosper economically in-world in whichever sector or sectors stimulate you. We also explore creating a Second Life presence for a real-life business, brand or service which may not strictly speaking be directly money-making but ultimately intends to boost business so is interpreted as such.

This book assumes that you are not a Second Life newbie. I assume you have resided in-world for at least a couple of months and that you have used at least some of this time to acquire a fairly good knowledge of Second Life terms, system requirements, viewer features and the basic building/texturing skills.

It is important to note that the intention of this volume is not to advocate a particular entrepreneurial path through Second Life but rather to give residents the real skills and tested strategies required to develop success wherever our imaginations may take us and whatever our dreams may be. My job is to hold your hand then guide you through the first few doors towards the ladder that is Second Life commercial success and in so doing serve to equip you with practical skills to climb and also help you to avoid many of the pitfalls, misunderstandings and delusions that befall so many residents. How high you climb this ladder will be solely up to your own imagination and industry.

Bon voyage.

Prie Tsure Xxx

acknowledgements

Little of my own learning would have been possible without considerable input from the many contributors to the Second Life Knowledgebase, The Second Life Wiki, the LSL Portal and the LSL Wiki.

I appreciate the hard work and time spent by my proofreaders cum technical advisers **Sandro Sonnenblume** and **Zib Scaggs**.

I thank my friends as well as the staff, DJs and members of the global 'Irie Vibes' community who collectively and daily inspire and motivate me to learn more, create more and provide more with their love, wit, wisdom, support, challenges and strengths.

I thank Linden Lab, their staff and the residents of Second Life for giving me a platform and a voice.

Finally but above all, I thank my family who, though often bewildered, support me with almost no question. I love you and learn most from you.

01

business in second life

In this chapter you will learn:

- about the Second Life economy
- about its marketplace and the the potential for income
- about intellectual property rights
- about the different business opportunities

The Second Life economy

The Second Life world utilizes the Linden dollar as its unit of currency. Residents use Linden dollars to pay for goods and services provided by other residents. The Linden dollar can also be legally exchanged for US dollars and other foreign currencies on a number of different websites including the LindeX™ exchange, and it is this fact that motivates many of us to explore the opportunity of generating a meaningful income from virtual trade.

Understanding the Second Life market

Most new residents are exploring and seeking experiences for stimulation but have little or no money to spend in Second Life. However, new residents are an important target market for businesses as they provide our traffic, but more importantly are the resource from which our long-term residents are produced. Converting a new resident into a long-term resident is simply a matter of providing and maintaining their engagement.

A long-term resident is an individual who has established and maintains a regular in-world presence. Long-term residents provide much of the colour, character and experience within Second Life, they are the trendsetters and the social fabric. These residents regularly require their own space as well as a whole world of products and services including clothing, accessories, homes and entertainment.

Who are the long-term residents? – Know your customers!

The socialites

Though people become long-term residents for a multitude of reasons, it is the social dimension of Second Life that is the feature seized upon by the majority residents. It is simple for new residents to quickly bond with a group of like-minded friends and become entwined within a rich social tapestry.

The excluded

The ability to access an unfettered second existence and to fully participate within such a vast social structure from the relative comfort of home provides an escape from isolation for many individuals challenged in real life by social exclusion, disability or illness. There are a considerable, disproportionate and rising number of socially excluded individuals finding comfort in Second Life both as fully integrated residents and as a functioning element of a global community.

The creatives

Building skills are easy to learn and enable residents to create an unending supply of objects ranging from intricate jewellery pieces to fully furnished mansion houses. Simple coding skills allow us to write scripts to give these objects functionality. Our creativity is also expressible with photography, video or Machinima. Established and emerging performers, DJs and musicians from all genres and all corners of the real world are also finding performance opportunities within Second Life.

The gamers

Second Life provides an almost limitless range of games to play. I can now play chess up close and personal with my Internet opponent while other residents choose to compete in grid-wide, themed or role-playing games. There are thousands of easy to find games listed every day in an easy to use search facility incorporated into the Second Life viewer.

Students and their teachers

Offering a platform for cooperative work, simulation and training, the Second Life grid provides a uniquely flexible platform for educators and students as well as allowing educational institutions to provide learning opportunities that offer a sense of presence and engagement to distant students who may otherwise feel isolated.

The entrepreneurs

At any given time there are tens if not hundreds of thousands of residents attempting to establish a business.

Real-life brands and businesses

Real-world brands already established on the Second Life grid include Nissan, Reuters, Orange and Sony BMG. As with the onset of the Internet itself, and as it becomes more probable that tens and perhaps hundreds of millions more Internet users will interact, shop and be entertained virtually, so forward-looking companies are now creating their in-world presences.

Charities and non-profit organizations

Charities, non-profit organizations and NGOs are utilizing Second Life by building in-world museums, libraries and facilities. The Second Life grid is a cost-effective global platform from which organizations can campaign and host events to both promote awareness and raise funds for their various causes.

What is the potential?

Offering value in goods and/or services to long-term Second Life residents provides potential for income. Every month, in excess of US$20,000,000 is exchanged between Second Life residents and by any measure this holds plenty of scope for earning. But we should be realistic about how much we can each expect to earn. If a resident wants to maximize their earning potential in-world with no financial outlay, and if they are willing to invest the necessary time then specializing in manufacture and retail can potentially earn US$500–1000 per month at the current level of residents.

The promise of a monthly income of a few hundred dollars may not reach the riches promised by the media but we still exist in the earliest days of virtual worlds. Many commentators predict exponential growth for Second Life over the coming years and if they are correct in these forecasts then in-world businesses that are successful today will be superbly placed to generate even more significant incomes in the future. But I like to deal with the landscape that we have, and in Second Life we currently have the potential to earn a few hundred dollars a month to start with. Also let us not forget that Second Life is a uniquely global phenomenon and within developing economies and many households this amount of additional income could not be considered insignificant.

Now is the moment to invest time and get involved for we may be at the very early stages of something extremely big!

For those businesses in which maximizing income is not the priority, I still maintain that the business should break even in-world and not become a financial burden to the owner. Any business that costs the resident money is an expensive hobby and in my experience is doomed to be abandoned. If your business doesn't make money then it is not functioning well and will be less fun and less fulfilling for you to operate.

Turning a profit is significant in several ways:

- Profit provides the inspiration to continue the project.
- Profit provides satisfaction and maintains realistic aspirations.
- Profit demonstrates a successful business model.
- Profit proves you are an entrepreneur.

Intellectual property rights

The Second Life terms of service grant to residents the copyright and intellectual property rights over original and personally created content. This means that we have in Second Life both the same protection that is afforded to real-world innovators and the legal channels to pursue anyone who dares to significantly copy our in-world creations.

By the same token, when it comes to creating content, residents should always be as original as possible in order to respect the intellectual property rights of others. But it is often pointed out (in my view correctly) that there is no such thing as a wholly original idea, only variations on existing ideas, so it makes sense that gleaning inspiration, ideas and solutions from real-world products or other residents' creations is not only acceptable but impossible to prevent. For example, creating a pair of training shoes inspired by the latest designs by Nike seems perfectly reasonable to me (for this happens in our real-world high-streets all the time), but reproducing a product and/or for example, putting the Nike logo or Swoosh on your Second Life product potentially leaves a resident open to real-world legal action whether they are selling the shoes or not!

Irie tip

Copyright law is complex and does vary between territories. Input the search term 'copyright law' (or similar) plus the name of your country into your preferred search engine to learn more about copyright law within your local territory.

Business opportunities

Opportunities in manufacture and retail

Most of Second Life's most profitable businesses create items for other residents to purchase and so if maximizing income is your priority then I would certainly suggest that you carefully examine manufacture and retail as the most direct route to reaching your goal.

The principal commercial benefit of manufacture and retail within Second Life is that once a resident has created an object of value, then selling identical copies bears neither manufacturing time nor stock/material costs.

Fashion

The fashion houses of Second Life clothe hundreds of thousands of avatars with their latest styles and designs. This is a big sector! Perhaps the biggest. Fashion evolves quickly and the most successful designers host rapidly expanding ranges of high quality and original garments in stores dotted across the grid.

Avatar accessories

Producing and retailing avatar accessories such as hair, shoes, skins, tattoos, jewellery, etc. also provides a significant source of income for many residents. Again, it is those diligent residents who work to improve and increase their range of original and high quality products who prove to be the most successful.

Buildings and accessories

Some of Second Life's biggest brands retail building and landscaping products for residential and business use. Prefab buildings, furniture, flora and fauna are just a few elements of a long list of resident requirements.

Animations

Realistic, high-quality animations are time-consuming to produce and so the few businesses that provide a wide variety of original high quality animations dominate this sector. However, animating as a skill is incredibly simple to learn and provides perhaps the clearest opportunity for the diligent and creative resident to establish themselves as a leading supplier. My assessment of the sector is that it is currently under-populated.

Business opportunities in scripting

Innovative scripting allows Second Life objects to perform useful and entertaining tasks and functions. The practised scripter, with a little imagination, can create wonderful solutions and amazing functionality within Second Life objects. LSL (Linden Scripting Language) scripting is currently shrouded in mystery for most residents, but in reality the basic principles take only a few moments to grasp (see Chapter 5). Proficient scripters often work together with gifted builders to produce high quality goods and also are hired by other residents in a freelance capacity to provide scripting solutions.

Opportunities in resorts and nightclubs

There are very few successful and profitable entertainment resorts in Second Life. Many residents try running a nightclub but personally I think it's perhaps the hardest business nut to crack. It appears so simple. Build, play music and people will come and come again. No they won't. And even if a few do arrive, a club by itself is unlikely to be self-financing.

A successful nightclub must provide a sense of community, act as the focus of a group or offer an extraordinary level of entertainment and preferably all three. A successful nightclub is neither a poor imitation of a more successful venue nor primarily a camping station (venues relying on camping for traffic fool no one and serve to dissuade long-term residents from visiting).

Opportunities in virtual land management and real estate

In a previous time Linden Lab offered new residents 'First Land' for L$512 for 512 sq. m., a price substantially below a market rate that at one time rose to L$25 per sq. m. This allowed a few residents to cheaply acquire vast tracts of land by creatively pooling the 'First Land' allowance of many, many accounts. Some individuals made relative fortunes and still reap the benefits. But those days are gone. Linden Lab abandoned the First Land facility in mid-2007.

Land prices have since fallen and stabilized at a more realistic level since those heady days. Land prices still do fluctuate and as such provide an opportunity for investors and speculators.

As well as price speculation, the Second Life real estate market provides opportunities for residents to establish their own residential communities and business locations.

Buying land then leasing space to other residents for residential or commercial usage is a viable business model but it should be noted that the initial investment, ongoing costs and uncertain return make this sector unattractive as a start-up project for many entrepreneurial residents.

Opportunities in professional services

Residents offer others a wide range of professional in-world services such as counselling, public relations, architecture, design, event organizing, DJing and writing, to name a few. Providing services for other residents is not usually a lucrative vocation as any service offered is unlikely to be rewarded with anything like an equivalent real-world fee.

Services are general personally provided and so the resident must be in attendance to provide a service. Therefore this sector does not offer the same opportunity as manufacture and retail for no cost/no presence replication.

A few service providers (most noticeably designers and architects) do command impressive sounding fees. I myself have been paid hundreds of thousands of Linden dollars to design and build regions for other residents, but when we judge these figures against an equivalent real-world payday then Second Life wages still compare poorly.

Residents who provide professional services often do so to introduce, share and/or practise their real-life skills in the exciting global marketplace that is Second Life. These residents may not presently command fortunes in fees but Second Life's leading service providers are certainly establishing themselves and stand well positioned to capitalize upon future growth and development.

Opportunities in adult entertainment

The sex and adult entertainment industry within Second Life is an early port of call for many, many residents of Second Life and with new residents arriving by the thousand every day and with virtual sex being an important feature of many long-term residents' experiences, business in this sector always appears to be strong. I'm no expert in the industry but would dare to suggest that all the rules relating to other business sectors apply here. Manufacturing and retailing of high quality and innovative sex-related clothing, avatar accessories, animations and objects should prove profitable for any hard-working resident. Building a venue to support a specific 'interest' or group presents few additional challenges and some advantages (specifically traffic) over other venue ideas. And perhaps providing 'professional' services in this sector provides the easiest path to an income for any resident (though is *not* being recommended by Irie Tsure!).

Summary

Building an enterprise in Second Life is not rocket science, but it isn't a gold-rush either. To me the golden rule of success is that your products or services must be original or an improvement on what already exists within the Second Life marketplace. You cannot produce or retail trash and expect residents to purchase it in any meaningful quantity. You can't throw up a black box or quickly copy another nightclub and expect your venue to flourish. What you can do, very quickly and cheaply, is to explore the Second Life marketplace. You can test the market with your products, venues and services to identify which concepts work and which don't. An entrepreneur should therefore evolve and develop. Start small, pay attention and follow then expand your businesses which perform well.

Always remember that however inspired your concept may feel, ultimately its success as a business will be decided by other Second Life residents.

02

creating retail objects

In this chapter you will learn:

- how to use the building grids and rulers
- about some prim variations
- about sculptured prims
- to apply flex and light properties to prims

Necessity is the mother of invention

Perhaps my favourite characteristic of the Second Life world is that without cost and with a little effort, I can create anything I need. I am a practised builder and now consider myself a proficient content creator. The reason for this is simple. Arriving with nothing, no money and no relevant skills, I have rarely been in the position financially to purchase what I require and therefore have usually needed to learn to produce those items that are not freely available.

The process takes time but without doubt offers the most certain way to:

- Learn, develop and practise a wide range of skills;

- Maintain freshness within your ideas;

- Create a wide range of products for retail purposes;

- Keep costs down and make a profit.

Objects in Second Life are constructed by altering and linking prims. I assume that you are familiar with the different prims types available and the ways in which they can be altered, repositioned and linked. If you are not then I suggest attacking those notecards you should have picked up on Help Island.

Impression

Much of the skill of building lies in creating a correct impression for the resident looking at the object. To make matters more complex for the content creator, most objects will be viewable from all angles and each resident's system and viewer settings will be set up differently. As such the craft involved in creating high quality representations takes a little time and experience to develop but can be approached in a couple of different ways.

An authentic impression can be created by being as accurate in the reproduction as is possible. The finished object is presented in-world as an accurate portrayal of a real-world object and it is both great fun and very satisfying to work on the detail of these largely artistic practice projects. The biggest problem with authentic representation is that such builds are complex and often require large numbers of prims in their construction. This is fine if you have plenty of land or have found a super sandbox, but unfortunately objects heavy in prims will often dissuade potential purchasers who may not have the necessary prim allowance to render the object on their own land. Prim count is less important when creating objects designed to be attached to residents as the prims do not count against parcel prim usage though it should be noted that high prim avatar attachments still add to server load and therefore help to create lag.

Alternatively, and in order to save prims, a 'sensed' impression is often created by attempting to create a fairly realistic representative of a real-world object but in doing so abandoning many of the authentic but superfluous details. Prim count is reduced by imaginative prim manipulation and clever use of texturing. An example of 'sensed impression' would be using transparency in a texture to create a one prim row of railings instead of creating each railing from prims.

Functionality

Functionality is crucial when designing and creating objects for Second Life and by functionality we are not discussing scripting right now. What I mean by functionality in this instance is contained in the answers to the two following questions:

1 Is the object practical?

If an avatar sits on a chair but their thighs protrude through the accompanying dining table, then the chair is not practical and functions poorly.

2 Will residents use the object?

If an avatar sits on a chair and the pose is basic, fixed and uninteresting then the avatar will usually stand up. Again the chair functions poorly.

Successful Second Life objects perform properly and are interesting.

High quality creativity within Second Life relies as much on our precision as it does on our imagination. We can be as creative as Monet but if we can't position our prims precisely then our work will still look a mess. Builders manage the accurate positioning and sizing of prims by using the rulers and grids provided within the Second Life viewer.

You should be familiar with these grids and rulers, but just in case you are not and as they are such crucial tools... here is a crash course:

The rulers and building grid

Ruler mode

From an object's **Edit** menu we can select **World, Local** or **Reference** from the **Ruler Mode** drop-down menu.

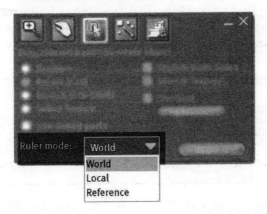

- **World** is the default ruler mode and when selected, irrespective of the object's orientation, the ruler and grid are displayed relative to the Second Life region. For example, when the object is in World ruler mode, dragging it along the red X axis will always move it east or west, in turn dragging the object along the green Y axis will always move it north or south and dragging it along the blue Z axis will always move the object vertically up or down. In the same way, when an object is in World ruler mode, rotating the object using the colour-coded rings will rotate the object around axes relative to the region.

- When **Local** ruler mode is selected, the ruler and grid are displayed relative to the current orientation of the selected object. For example, when in Local ruler mode, dragging an object along the X axis will move it forward or backwards relative to its current orientation, in turn, dragging an object along the Y axis will move it from side to side relative to its orientation and dragging it along the Z axis will still move it up and or down but now relative to its own orientation. When an object is in Local ruler mode, using the colour-coded rings rotates the object around its own local X, Y and Z axes.

- The **Reference** ruler mode does appear to be very useful but I'm not sure I've used it to provide a practical solution (yet). When the Reference ruler mode is selected, typing [**Shift**] + [**G**] fixes a reference grid based on the object's current coordinates and orientation. Whilst in this mode, further rulers and grids will be orientated to these reference coordinates and axes irrespective of the orientation of the next selected object.

Irie tip

It is best to reposition your view to drag objects from side to side or up and down. Dragging a prim towards or away from the camera position runs the risk of losing control of the movement and the object disappearing off into the distance.

The building grid

There is no better way to maintain perfection and develop building speed than with proficient use of the grid. In this instance we are not discussing the Second Life grid but instead the Second Life viewer's building grid. This allows builders to resize prims quickly to specific measurements and position objects rapidly to precise coordinates and orientations.

To use the building grid we must tick the **Use Grid** checkbox on the **Edit** menu ([**Ctrl**] + [**3**]). The building grid increments, and how far the grid extends, can both be adjusted by clicking the **Options...** button beneath the **Use Grid** checkbox.

By axis

When we are using the building grid, as soon as we start to drag an object along an axis by selecting one of the colour-coded handles, a ruler appears either side of the selected axis.

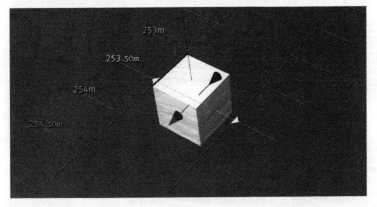

Move the cursor into either ruler to snap the prim into precise positions

An object will move freely along an axis when we drag it by its positional handle. Free movement occurs when the cursor remains between the two rulers. However if we drag the cursor into either ruler, then drag the object, it will incrementally and precisely snap along the axis between the ruler's marks. As the cursor drops back between the rulers, free movement is restored.

By plane

When an object is selected and depending on your view, up to three twin-colour triangles, the object's 'grid handles', appear in between the axis lines.

An object's grid handles permit us to move the object in increments simultaneously along two planes. As soon as we select a

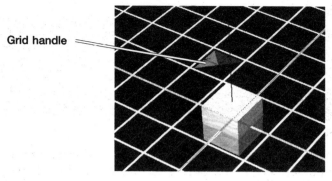

Grid handle

grid handle, the building grid will appear on the relevant plane and when we move the selected object it will snap precisely to this grid.

By rotation

Builders also use a ruler to precisely rotate their objects. As soon as we start to rotate an object around an axis by selecting one of the colour-coded axis rings, a ruler appears around the axis ring indicating the degrees of rotation around the selected object. When we move the cursor into this ruler, our object will rotate in increments making it easier to be precise.

By scale

Builders also use a ruler to precisely stretch or scale their objects. As soon as we start to scale an object by selecting one of the colour-coded scaling cubes, a ruler appears either side of the selected axis, making it easier to be precise as we stretch or scale.

Useful prim shapes

To confidently approach creating content, builders must firstly be equipped with the knowledge of which prims are available and into what subsequent shapes these prims can be altered. This allows us to approach a build armed with the information we need to best create all the shapes we will require to create high quality content.

The following shapes may not be obvious at first examination but are incredibly useful prim variations.

Cube family variations

The Cube prim is the foundation block of most Second Life building and its variations are pretty obvious in the main. However there are a few less apparent variations we should explore.

Hollowing out a cube then editing the Path Cut can save prims when creating regular shaped spaces for rooms, stores, etc.

1   Create a box then snap it to the world grid on at least the X and Y axis (keyboard shortcut [**Shift**] + [**X**]).

Irie tip

Whenever I build I ensure that the first prim I lay down is a regular sized cube and 'snapped to the World Grid', usually on all 3 axes but always at least on both the X and Y axes and also orientated (rotation) to 0,0,0. A regularly positioned foundation prim acts as a ruler for all the other prims I wish to position and will allow for simple but perfect alignment.

---

2   From the **Edit** menu select the **Object** tab then Hollow out your cube by 95%.

3   Snap rotate the cube on the Y axis to 270°.

4   From the **Edit** menu select the **Object** tab and edit **Path Cut B** to 0.20.

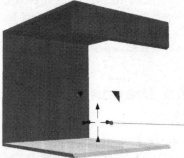

5   Copy this prim then position both prims on identical coordinates. The simplest way to achieve this is to hold [**Shift**] then drag the object along any axis. A copy will be rendered on the same position. Use [**Ctrl**] + [**Y**] (Undo) to reposition the original prim back in its original position.

6 Rotate one of the prims back to 0,0,0.

7 Edit the **Path Cut B** of this prim to 0.25.

8 Select both prims ([**Shift**] + click) and link them ([**Ctrl**] + [**L**]).

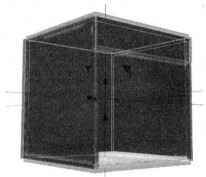

This object becomes the two-prim base of the functional and low-prim modular store system that I use in our shopping malls. By making these stores 10m × 10m × 8–10m and positioning the first store carefully on the world grid, I can very simply copy, reposition and perfectly align, stores as required. This design also allows for effortless store modification, for example, I can open up two adjacent stores simply by editing the relevant prims' path cut.

I created this modular store system using only a few cubes. The columns are cubes that have been stretched on the Z axis then twisted. Small alterations were used to eliminate Z flutter (the nasty flickering of textures where prims overlap) but I was careful not to reduce the overall and regular exterior dimensions of each module as this would have left untidy gaps between the prims. (See Chapter 3, Advanced texturing.)

Modular building elements should be designed to use regular dimensions and orientations so perfect alignment is always simple. Use the Grid!

One-prim steps

A pair of steps can be carved from a single cube prim in the following manner:

1 Edit a box from the Object tab by setting the Path Cut Begin to **0.125** and Path Cut End to **0.875**. (*Remember these values; you will use them a lot!*)

2 Rotate and stretch the prim as required.

Rounding corners

Rounding a corner can make many builds appear smoother, more professional and ultimately more pleasing on the eye. To round a corner:

1 Edit a box in the **Object** tab by setting the **Path Cut Begin** to 0.125 and **Path Cut End** to 0.875.

2 [Shift] + drag a copy and then from the **Object** tab, change the Building Block Type to Cylinder.

3 Edit this cylinder in the **Object** tab by setting the **Path Cut Begin** to 0.5 and **Path Cut End** to 0.75.

4 [Ctrl] + [Z] should reposition this prim perfectly aligned with the cut cube and provide a smooth curved corner (use the Grid to align if necessary).

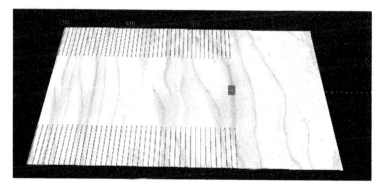

Hollowed and rounded

A big prim

For low-prim environments flattening a 10m × 10m cube to its minimum (Z axis to 0.01) and then editing the Top Shear on the X and/or Y axis creates a single prim that appears to extend beyond the 10m limits of a normal prim.

Spirals

A simple and single-prim spiral ramp or 'staircase' is shaped by rendering a cylinder then twisting it from B to 180 and E to –180. Edit Path Cut B to 0.98 and Path Cut E to 1.00.

Corkscrew-type shapes are created by twisting cubes then tapering them (and also hollowing them if we wish to). When hollowing, remember not to automatically use the default hole shape. Variety can often be used to add the visual spice of interest to your building.

Sphere variations

At first inspection, variations of spheres do appear pretty basic. Path cutting and hollowing offer useful but predictable segment shapes and dimpling combined with hollowing allows builders to 'open' the sphere, producing useful cup and vase shapes. But the sphere variations get really interesting when twisting is applied and even more so when combining twist with varying degrees of dimpling and/or path cutting. Beyond art and ribbon bows, it becomes difficult for me to give you examples of the practical usage of this multitude of seemingly abstract shapes, but these shapes delight my eye so experiment with them and please let me know the practical applications you discover.

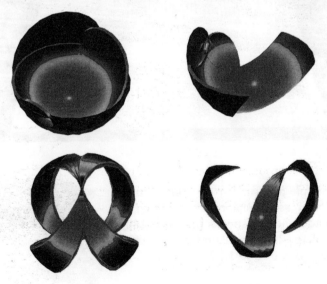

Torus variations

I'd never heard of a 'torus' until I got here, but as a builder I quickly fell in love with the shape as it produces the most organic and natural looking prims that I have yet discovered within the Second Life default prim types (my sculptures contain more tori than any other prim type).

Horn, spiral and claw shapes can be simply produced by tapering a torus then applying some revolutions if necessary. Hollowing these shapes then editing the hole sizes produces even more amazing tori variations.

> ### Irie tip
>
> **Twisting a torus to 90° on both B and E will create a more natural-looking cushion.**

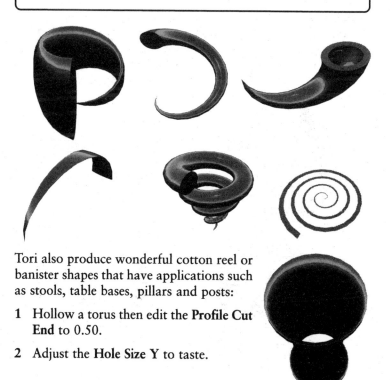

Tori also produce wonderful cotton reel or banister shapes that have applications such as stools, table bases, pillars and posts:

1   Hollow a torus then edit the **Profile Cut End** to 0.50.

2   Adjust the **Hole Size Y** to taste.

You will find it helpful to your progress to experiment with tori using different path cuts, hollow sizes and hollow shapes. Various twists, shears, profile cuts, revolutions and radii can also be applied in different combinations to create an almost infinite variety of amazing prim variations.

Tube variations

The single prim table or stool

To produce a single prim stool:

1 Render a tube.

2 Edit **Hole Size Y** to 0.50.

3 Edit **Profile Cut B** to 0.25 and **Profile Cut E** to 0.95.

4 Stretch/scale to taste.

5 Carve out the stool by editing **Hollow** to 80.

To produce a single prim table:

1 Render a tube.

2 Edit **Hole Size Y** to 0.50.

3 Edit **Profile Cut B** to 0.15 and **Profile Cut E** to 0.90.

4 Hollow, stretch and scale to taste.

The single prim stool or table has several individual faces that for maximum effect we should take the time to texture individually.

Ring variations

The usual method employed to produce a vehicle wheel is to flatten a cylinder. The result is rather uninspiring. Try this instead:

1 Render a ring.

2 Edit **Twist B** to 90 and **Twist E** to 90.

3 Edit **Profile Cut B** to taste (e.g. 0.10).

4 Edit **Profile Cut E** to taste (e.g. 0.75).

5 Hollow to 20(%).

We can also make dishes, containers, etc. using this method and a similar more rounded variation can be produced by in the first instance rendering a torus instead of a ring.

Irie tip

Experimenting and familiarizing yourself with prim variations is essential for proficient building. Knowing the shapes that are available enables us to solve most creative problems quickly and prim-efficiently.

Sculpted prims

Sculpted prims are used to create more complex, organic shaped prims that are not possible with the default prim system. A sculpted prim's shape is described by the RGB (Red, Green, Blue) values in an image file (a Sculpt Texture or Sculpt Map) which as a result appears as a strangely beautiful rainbow texture.

Currently, I create sculpted prims externally using the free 3D modelling software Blender (www.blender.org) and Wings 3D (www.wings3d.com). I then convert the model into a Second Life sculpt map (using an exporter plug-in) and upload this into Second Life (as an image file). The imported sculpt map is applied to a prim from its **Object** tab by selecting **Sculpted** from the **Building Block Type** dropdown menu then selecting the new sculpt texture using the **Sculpt Texture** panel.

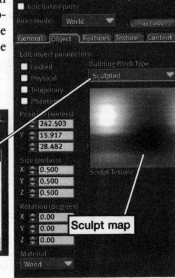

Wings 3D is easy to learn and well suited for making sculpted prims. You will find the sculpt map exporter plug-in for Wings 3D by entering the search-term 'sculpty exporter for Wings 3D' or similar into your preferred search engine. This enables us to produce a Second Life sculpt map directly from the 3D modelling software.

If you get more involved with creating sculpted prims there is little doubt that you will want to put the time and effort into learning the more complex Blender software (or similar). Free and with all the features of the expensive programs, Blender is my preferred software. However, be warned, Blender does take some time and effort to master though both the manual and tutorials are available online from the Blender website.

To get a sense of what is possible with sculpted prims take a look in the *library* folder of your inventory and you will find some excellent examples of sculpted prim creations. This wonderfully detailed sculpted fruit bowl by Qarl Linden is in there.

Irie prediction

I have little doubt that in the not too distant future, solutions for creating sculpted prims in-world will become freely available.

Prim features

The *features* of flexibility and light can be applied to prims in order to enhance their functionality, effect and authenticity.

Irie note

Prim features must be applied to individual prims, therefore when working on a linked group, the **Edit linked parts** checkbox must be ticked and then a single prim selected prior to applying the desired feature.

Adding flexible properties to a prim

Assigning flexible or *flexi* properties to prims adds an enormous degree of dynamism and realism to objects such as flags, prim clothing, flora, etc. With flexi applied, these objects appear floppy and react to both Second Life gravity and wind.

Irie note

Flexi prims are always Phantom in nature and additionally cannot have their Physics parameter enabled.

We assign the various flexible properties to a prim by initially ticking the **Flexible Path** checkbox found on the **Features** tab of the selected prim's **Edit** menu then adjusting the various values within the input fields beneath.

Features
Edit object features:
☑ Flexible Path
Softness ⇕ 2.000
Gravity ⇕ 0.300
Drag ⇕ 2.000
Wind ⇕ 0.000
Tension ⇕ 1.000
Force X ⇕ 0.000
Force Y ⇕ 0.000
Force Z ⇕ 0.000

Exploration and discovery will prove your best strategy to grasp the effects of applying varying degrees of the following flexible path properties. Flexi properties are easiest to observe on stretched prims such as the elongated cube used in the above image.

- **Softness** is applied in whole number values ranging from 0 to 3. A softness value of 0 results in a very solid and erect prim whilst entering a softness value of 3 results in a prim that behaves more like wet lettuce.

- **Gravity** is applied in values ranging from –10.0 to +10.0. The gravity value dictates the degree of downward force (or upward force for negative values) exerted on the prim with the value of 0.0 being weightlessness or zero gravity.

- **Drag** is applied in values from 0.0 to +10.0. The value dictates how air friction affects the movement. A value of 0.0

results in a very 'whippy' prim while one of 10.0 results in the prim responding in a more relaxed and flowing manner.

- **Wind** is applied in values ranging from 0.0 to +10.0. The value dictates how the prim is affected by the wind's strength and direction. A value of 0.0 results in a no reaction to wind whilst a value of 10.0 results in the prim responding wildly to the wind as though it were made of tissue paper.

- **Tension** is applied in values ranging from 0.0 to 10.0. The tension value dictates how much stiffness is applied to the prim. A tension value of 0.0 results in a very floppy prim whilst a tension value of 10.0 results in a very stiff prim.

- **Force X, Y, Z** is applied in values ranging from –10.0 to +10.0. The value dictates the degree of directional force exerted on the prim with 0.0 being neutral. It allows us to apply a directional force to a flexi prim, and is perfect when we want to allow a prim to flutter in the breeze, but only in a certain direction, e.g. to keep hanging curtains away from seating.

Irie tip

To see how a flexi prim reacts we need to move it. To save time while you explore the flexible properties, rather than repeatedly dragging the prim around, move it once then move it as you require using [Ctrl] + [Z] and [Ctrl] + [Y].

Adding light properties to a prim

Assigning light properties allows us to create objects that both radiate light and illuminate the surrounding environment.

We cause a prim to emit light by ticking the **Light** checkbox found on the **Features** tab of the selected prim's **Edit** menu, selecting a colour from the **Color** *[sic]* palette then adjusting the various values within the input fields beneath.

☑ Light	
Color	
Intensity	1.000
Radius	10.000
Falloff	0.750

As always, experimentation will prove the best method to grasp the effects of applying varying degrees of the light properties.

• **Color** [*sic*] is applied to the light with a click on the panel then selecting a colour from the displayed colour picker. Changing the colour of the emitted light often changes the colour of the object.

• **Intensity** dictates how much light is emitted from the prim and is applied to the light in values ranging between 0.000 (no light) and 1.000 (max. light).

• **Radius** dictates the reach of the emitted light and is set by inputting a value between 0.000 and 20.000 metres. The path of the light emitted from a prim is not interrupted by objects such as walls and floors therefore we use radius to restrict a light's spread.

• **Falloff** applies a diminishing intensity gradient along the light's path in values between 0.000 and 2.000. A value of 0.000 applies no falloff and the light will display at full intensity within the entire radius. A value of 2.000 applies maximum falloff and the light intensity quickly diminishes towards the radius.

Irie's building tips

- **Be diligent.** In order to broaden your building 'vocabulary', take the time to explore prim variations and features, learn new skills and then practise them.

- **Build as you require.** Save money and learn at the same time. If you need a new sofa then build a new sofa!

- **Be innovative.** Improve objects that are available and develop products that are not.

- **Use the building grid.** Build precisely by using the rulers and building grid provided, wherever possible.

- **Build using regularly sized prims.** When practical, build using prims of regular dimensions (1.0m, 1.25m, 5.0m, etc.) and placed at regular angles (0°, 45°, 90°, etc.) to make the positioning, aligning and texturing of prims a simple process.

- **Become a perfectionist.** Do not tolerate unintentional gaps, overlaps or other errors in your building.

- **Build in good light.** Fix the sun to an appropriate position to build your object then view it under different lighting conditions (e.g. **World > Environment Settings > Midday**).

- **Build a module library.** When you create a building element that either you particularly like or feel could be useful again then link it into a single object, name it well then take a copy of the object into your inventory.

- **Set the perms.** Never transfer an object to another resident without carefully checking that you are comfortable with the state of the item permissions.

- **Check functionality.** Create an Alt (alternative account) to check the object works as intended with other avatars.

- **Remain at the cutting edge.** Take the time to keep abreast of Second Life's new tools and features via the Second Life blog. Visit other creators' stores and view their content to glean their latest thinking and solutions.

- **Become part of the creative community.** Second Life permits, no encourages, us to surround ourselves with creative individuals. Chat with and engage those content creators you admire and also those residents (like us) who aspire to create high quality objects.

03 advanced texturing

In this chapter you will learn:

- how to capture in-world images
- how to incorporate transparency into a texture
- how to texture effectively

Perfectly applying high quality textures is well worth both the effort and the time it takes. Many a quality build is rendered practically worthless by poor texturing and whatever items we poorly texture also leaves open the door for our product to be vastly improved by other more diligent residents.

Don't bother buying textures! Acquiring a wide range of textures is managed by visiting the freebie stores and your inventory library. Walls, floors, fabrics, organic textures, etc. are widely available in-world and are both full-perm and copyright free.

Irie note

A 'texture' is any uploadable *.tga, *.bmp, *.jpg, *.jpeg or *.png file which can be captured in-world, sourced using other methods or created using non-Second Life software.

As your building and texturing becomes more advanced you will soon require textures that you cannot find free of charge. You can buy textures in-world if you wish but you will find it more rewarding to source and/or produce your own.

Capturing in-world textures

An example of the practical application of a texture created in-world would be when we need to create an image to be used within a sign or vendor, e.g. we want to overlay some text and maybe incorporate another image with an in-world snapshot to advertise our product or service.

The obvious method to create a texture in-world is by using the Snapshot feature of the Second Life viewer. Depending on the required image, the following functions and effects can be explored to assist you in capturing the highest quality shots.

Irie note

Adjusting some of these settings is likely to have a horrible impact on your system performance so do not forget to reset these settings when you have finished taking snapshots.

Ultra

To attain the highest level of detail whilst taking snapshots, I always set the graphics preferences ([Ctrl] + [P] > **Graphics** tab) to **Ultra** and then check the **Custom** box to set the draw distance to an appropriate level of detail. For the image on page 36 the viewer's draw distance was set to 512m.

High-res Snapshot

When you are taking snapshots, and assuming that you have the required space on your hard drive, I recommend selecting the **High-res Snapshot** preference from the **Advanced** menu ([Ctrl] + [Alt] + [D]). Working with high resolution images is useful for maintaining definition when cropping or applying other edits or effects.

Take snapshots to disk

To ensure that I am satisfied with the result I save all my snapshots to my hard drive so I can check, crop and edit the image before spending the L$10 to upload the texture to the Second Life servers.

Irie tip

Use the keyboard shortcut [Ctrl] + ['] to quickly and easily save several snapshots to your hard drive.

Disable Camera Constraints

Selecting the **Disable Camera Constraints** option in the **Advanced** menu ([Ctrl] + [Alt] + [D]) allows for unrestricted movement when using the camera controls.

Anisotropic Filtering

Anisotropic filtering renders more distinct edges on distant objects. To enable it, click the **Hardware Options** button found on **Preferences** > **Graphics** tab then tick the **Anisotropic Filtering** checkbox.

Zoom In and Out

Zoom In ([Ctrl] + [0]) is useful for stepping repeatedly closer to a subject while **Zoom Out** ([Ctrl] + [8]) can be used to incorporate wider angle scenes and panoramas. **Zoom Default** ([Ctrl] + [9]) resets the camera view.

Lighting

Select the **Nearby local lights** radio button, after ticking the **Custom** checkbox on the **Graphics** tab of the **Preferences** window, to cast light from the six nearest light sources. We can add contrast, tone and depth to a scene by enabling light features on prims then positioning them as lamps, carefully and close by our subject.

Environment Editor

From **World > Environment Settings > Environment Editor** we have the ability to reposition the sun as well as dramatically alter the appearance and colour of Second Life's sky and water (in your viewer only). Click on the **Advanced Sky** and **Advanced Water** buttons and experiment with the settings to find the best look for your snapshot.

Hide the User Interface

Selecting [Ctrl] + [Alt] + [F1] (or **Advanced > Rendering > Features > UI**) before taking a snapshot will give you an uninterrupted view of Second Life. After taking a snapshot, the UI (User Interface) will automatically display again.

Irie note

When using [Ctrl] + [Alt] + [F1], the UI is hidden, and not minimized. Be careful because hidden buttons can still be clicked!

Capture Modes

Alternative capture modes are available through the **Capture:** menu on the **Snapshot Preview** window. Capture modes are only available when **Save snapshot to hard drive** is selected and are most usually used when post-processing or editing images.

Colors

Normal mode looks like this.

The **Depth** mode is wonderful for silhouette style images and also useful when applying an effect (e.g. blur) to different depths within a scene.

The **Object Mattes** mode is useful for masking individual objects for precise editing.

Wireframe

[Ctrl] + [Shift] + [R] (or **Advanced menu > Rendering > Wireframe**) displays an interesting 'Matrix' style rendering of the Second Life world.

Joystick Flycam

Selecting **Advanced > Flycam** from the top menu-bar activates the Flycam feature and opens the **Flycam Options** window. For residents with a compatible joystick (or similar device) connected to their system, Flycam can be a useful tool for framing the viewer. Second Life also offers formal support for 3Dconnexion's SpaceNavigator 3D mouse.

Irie tip

Alternatively we can finely adjust the framing of the viewer using the in-built Camera Controls by selecting **View > Camera Controls** from the viewer's top menu bar.

Auto-snapshot

Ticking the **Auto-snapshot** checkbox on the **Snapshot Preview** window facilitates taking several pictures quickly and in succession. When Auto-snapshot is enabled, clicking the **Save** button not only saves the previous shot but also captures a new image. Clicking the **New Snapshot** button instead of the **Save** button discards the current image.

Full Screen

We usually run Second Life in a window to make it simple to switch between different open applications. But to capture the largest possible screen area we clear the **Run Second Life in a window** checkbox from **Preferences > Graphics** tab and run the viewer full screen.

Print Screen

Occasionally when wishing to capture an image containing certain UI (user interface) items, taking a snapshot within the Second Life viewer becomes impractical. **[Print Screen]** on the keyboard copies the screen image to the clipboard and we can then paste it into any appropriate application for cropping and/or editing.

We use these snapshot features and settings to create high-definition imagery

Acquiring real-world textures

From the Internet

The Image Search feature of your preferred search engine will provide you with an unending supply of textures. Though copyright law precludes us from copying and reproducing many of the images we find, there are thousands of 'royalty-free' image and texture libraries available on the Internet. Enter the term 'royalty free image', 'copyright free image' or similar into your preferred search engine.

We should not use copyright or trademarked material in Second Life as the rightful owner of an image can take direct legal action against us in real-world courts of law.

Infringement of copyright only occurs where either the whole or a substantial part of an image is used without permission. The term 'substantial part' is not defined under copyright law but has been interpreted by the courts to mean a significant part of the work. This means that a small (and to be safe, insignificant and unidentifiable) region of an image may be copied and reproduced without any risk of infringing a copyright. For example if you needed a water texture you could safely scan and use an area of sea from Colour plate 1 without seeking my permission or infringing my copyright. This 'free use' allows us to produce an infinite variety of useful textures.

Digital cameras

To eliminate any consideration of copyright infringement you may wish to take your own pictures. When you need a new brick texture just go outside into the real world and take a photo. You will normally wish to ensure that the camera is at perfect right-angles to the subject to maintain the correct perspective.

Editing textures

The practical advantage of saving images to disk is so that we can edit them. To crop, resize, scale, add text, etc. to an image, we must employ a stand-alone (i.e. non-Second Life) software package.

With luck your system already contains basic picture editing software such as MS Picture Editor, MS Paint or iPaint. These products are useful for cropping and resizing, and fulfil our basic editing needs. However, you will in all likelihood quickly wish to progress your editing using more complex features unavailable in these basic packages. If you are fortunate enough to already own software such as Paint Shop Pro or PhotoShop then great; otherwise there is GIMP. This is the wonderful, freely downloadable open-source program that I use for photo retouching, image composition and image authoring. GIMP (www.gimp.org) is an acronym for GNU Image Manipulation Program and has been written and developed to run on both MS Windows and the Mac OS. It is simple to learn and I love it!

Adding text to an image

Adding text to an image can be managed by using your preferred picture editing software (e.g. GIMP). A simpler but more versatile method I use to incorporate text into an image is to compose the image using the WordArt feature in MS Office.

Within Microsoft Word, PowerPoint, etc. are these functions to insert images and decorative text:

- Insert > Picture > from File

- Insert > Picture > WordArt

WordArt is the MS Office feature that allows for creative text editing using your system's own font library.

To group and save these insertions as one uploadable image, we select all the elements of the finished composition (using [Shift] + [A]) then right-click and select **Save as Picture** from the drop down menu. We save the image as a .bmp (recommended) file either for further editing or for uploading to Second Life.

Select All, right-click then Save as Picture...

Using transparency

Creating transparent areas in an image is an important texturing skill to master. We incorporate transparency not only to allow skin to show through for makeup, tattoo and clothing textures but also for effective and prim-efficient building.

For example, these barbed wire and chain-link fences were produced as textures by selecting the white spaces between the 'wires' on the original image then making these spaces transparent.

Within Second Life, only the *.tga and *.png file formats can display transparency and so the more basic picture editing packages become unsuitable. I will always encourage residents to accumulate their hard-earned money so the following transparency tutorial is based around the free GIMP software.

I wish to add our logo to our advertisement but the logo file has a grey background that I will need to make transparent first. (Yes I know that it would be simpler to use the circular selection tool within GIMP to copy and paste the required region into the advertisement, but in this instance we are using this method purely as an example of how to create transparent regions of the texture.)

1 Open the image file in the GIMP software.

2 Select **Layer > Transparency > Add Alpha Channel** from the top menu (within GIMP).

Irie note

The Alpha Channel is required to produce and display transparency.

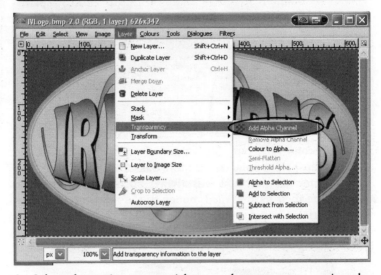

3 Select the regions you wish to make transparent using the most appropriate selection tool from the GIMP Toolbox. We may select by shape, colour or draw our own selection. Here I will select the grey regions using the Magic Wand which selects adjacent (contiguous) regions of the same colour. Holding down [Shift] then left-clicking further regions adds them to our selection.

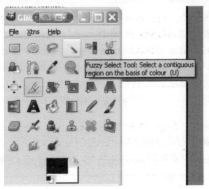

4 Once the region(s) you wish to make transparent have been selected, select **Layer > Transparency > Colour to Alpha** from the top menu (of GIMP). The transparent areas will be shown in a shades of grey checker board design in a preview window. Assuming that you are happy with the selected regions click **OK** on this preview window.

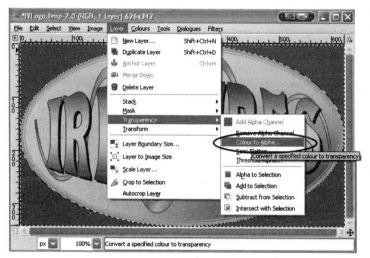

5 Save the image as either:

A TarGA file (*.tga): Use **File > Save As...**, open the **Select File Type (By Extension)** menu then select the Targa image file extension. Click **Save**.

Or

A PNG file (*.png): Use **File > Save As...**, open the **Select File Type (By Extension)** menu then select the PNG image file extension. Click **Save** and a **Save as PNG** window will open. Clear the **Save background colour** option then click **Save**.

Irie note

Unlike TarGA files, PNG transparency does not save the alpha channel. A .png file size will therefore be smaller than a .tga file and the texture will be quicker to load in-world.

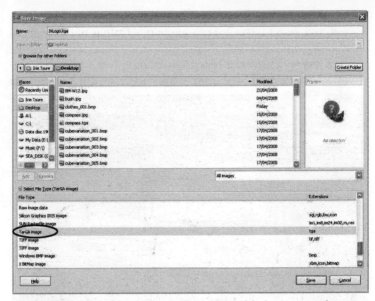

This logo texture is now ready to be added to our advertisement.

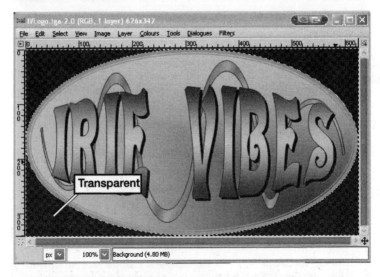

We then open our original image file in GIMP, insert our new TarGA or PNG logo file (**File > Open as Layer**) then resize and position the image as necessary.

Finally we give the image a name and save it in our preferred format. I usually save as *.png as the PNG format not only gives me the transparency option but also a great compromise between the larger (slower to load in-world) higher quality TarGA and BMP formats and the smaller but less defined JPEG format.

Our finished texture

Advanced texture editing

It is a sensible strategy to familiarize yourself with the functionality of your chosen image editing software package. The more extensive your knowledge of the functions and effects they can produce then the more effective your editing will be. Practise, practise and practise!

Editing a texture for upload

The Second Life viewer allows us to upload the following formats of image files. I have placed them in order of my personal preference for Second Life usage.

1 **.png** – small file size, high quality, can handle transparency

2 **.tga** – larger files, high quality, can handle transparency

3 **.bmp** – larger files, high quality, cannot handle transparency

4 **.jpg/.jpeg** – small file size, lower quality and no transparency.

Irie note

The Second Life viewer converts images to JPG2000. Avoid saving your work as a jpeg as the image quality may be reduced due to the double jpeg conversion.

Uploading textures to Second Life

When we upload a texture to the Second Life servers it will be resized square and in a power of 2 (i.e. 16 × 16 pixels, 32 × 32, 64 × 64, etc.). It is therefore good practise to resize a texture to one of these sizes prior to upload to avoid unexpected distortion by maintaining absolute control over the aspect.

The maximum resolution for an uploaded texture is set at 1024 × 1024 pixels. When we upload any texture of higher resolution it will be automatically resized to 1024 × 1024 pixels.

Uploading images to the Second Life servers is as simple as selecting **File > Upload Image** from the viewer's top menu bar then browsing for the required image file (I usually save images to the Desktop for simple location). There is a L$10 charge levied by Linden Lab for each uploaded image. The uploaded texture(s) can be found in the inventory's *Texture* folder and are located most easily using its **Recent Items** filter.

To upload files as a batch we select **File > Bulk Upload** from the Second Life viewer's top menu bar. We select the files we want to upload by holding down **[Ctrl]** then clicking their filenames.

Using textures effectively

I feel that I cannot stress too often or too strongly that poor or lazy texturing can completely ruin otherwise superb building and wonderful creativity.

The following example has all the correct textures on all the correct surfaces but no texture editing has been applied and therefore my store looks a mess.

Examples of poor texturing may include (but are not limited to):

◆ Z flutter caused when two prim surfaces are occupying the same plane

◆ Stretched or incorrectly scaled textures

◆ Incorrectly rotated textures

◆ Incorrectly mapped textures

◆ Texture seams

◆ Glare on light surfaces.

Select texture

Unless we are texturing a default cube it is likely that we will need to edit different faces individually in order for the object to appear in the correct proportion and perspective.

A prim may have up to nine faces (see the hollowed and path-cut cube on page 48) each of which can (and often should) be individually textured. Selecting the **Select Texture** radio button on the **Texture** tab permits each face to be edited using any of the functions on that tab.

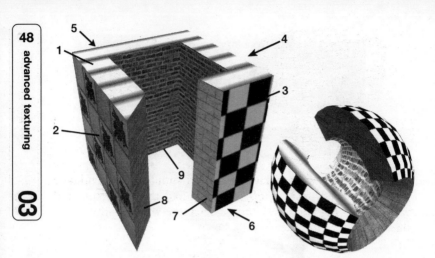

Any surfaces inside a hollowed prim are considered as a single face

Texture mapping

As our building becomes more practised we are more and more likely to be using prims that we have edited. Editing the shape of a prim can cause the texture to appear scaled, seamed and/or distorted.

For example, to correct the distorted texture from this tapered cube prim, select **Planar** from the **Mapping** drop-down menu and our texture is then applied uniformly to the plane of the prim rather than compressed within the proportions of prim surfaces.

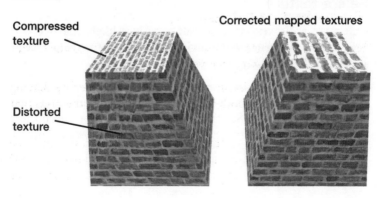

Compressed
texture

Corrected mapped textures

Distorted
texture

Each differently shaped face of a prim should be individually textured, scaled, resized, offset as required then shininess and planar mapping applied in order to explore which options produce the most effective result.

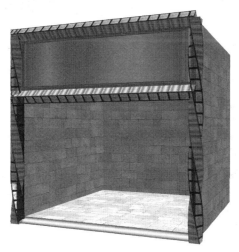

Texturing solutions

From the previous store module example I improved the texturing using the following techniques:

1 The Z-flutter previously visible has been removed by shaving a centimetre from both the width and depth of the prim that includes the floor.

2 The inside of both of the main prims is considered one face andso the texture previously appeared stretched over the four internal planes. To correct this we increase the 'Repeats Per

Face' of this surface to 4 and rotate through 90° the texture of the internal face of the prim element containing the floor.

3 As the vertical planes on the twisted columns are 20 times taller than the width (i.e. 10m × 0.5m) the texturing of the columns (including the horizontal columns positioned above and below the front panel) appeared very stretched. Increasing the Repeats Per Face to 20 on the vertical axis corrected the scale.

4 The prim containing the floor was given some grey colouring to help reduce glare from the light floor surface.

5 The front panel has been scaled and offset to fit a 1 × 1 texture within the visible area of this panel.

6 The surface revealed as the floor threshold was textured with a colour gradient running horizontally. This texture was rotated through 90° in order that the gradient runs vertically and therefore will appear consistently across several store modules.

Texturing sculpted prims

A sculpted prim has just one texture face. Any texture can be applied to this face using the prim's Texture tab. Experiment between default and planar mapping as planar mapping can appear better as with this sculpted hair-wrap.

Sculpted prims tend to be irregularly shaped and unlike my simple hair-wrap, a single sculpted prim may need to represent more than one type of material. For example, part of a sculpted prim may be metal; while another part may be wood. This makes texturing sculpted prims a complicated process.

3D programs such as Maya and ZBrush import the sculpted prim into the program and allow a texture to be created directly on its surface. The problem is that these programs are not free or cheap.

Surface textures for sculpted prims can also be produced using Blender and you should easily find online tutorials describing various (reasonably complicated but accurate) methods. An alternative more haphazard technique is to work on the texture in your preferred graphics software (e.g. GIMP) then use your preferred 3D modelling software (e.g. Wings 3D) to periodically preview the texture, note errors then return to GIMP to make the necessary adjustments. This hit and miss method is not as simple as painting directly onto a sculpted prim of course, but can prove a handy strategy for texturing the occasional sculpted prim as the only cost is time.

> ### Irie prediction
>
> I have little doubt that in the not too distant future free and simple software for texturing sculpted prims will become freely available.

Texturing summary

Human vision relies on its experience and belief of how the world should look and highlights any discrepancies within the patterns it expects to see. Accurate texturing therefore becomes essential to avoid great work looking shoddy. We may spend longer texturing an object than we have on building it and in the ultimate analysis this effort will almost always have proved to be worthwhile. It is not unusual for me to revisit every surface of a build to produce near perfect texturing. I will ensure consistent scale across all surfaces. I will view my object in different light settings and from different angles to see how it looks. I may apply shiny, full bright, varying degrees of transparency and/or glow etc. to surfaces to explore potential visual improvements. But I will do all of this at the very end of a building project. Do not spend time texturing until your build is complete. Why spend time acquiring, producing or working on the texture of a prim that you may well need to replace or edit further? The refining of your texturing is the final part of the building process.

04

creating fashion items

In this chapter you will learn:

- about clothing templates and texture mapping
- how to creating clothing items using graphics software
- how to create prim hair
- how to create Second Life shoes

Clothing

The potential

Almost every resident wants their avatar to appear stylish in one way or another and therefore many of Second Life's highest earners are the creators of fashion lines and brands. If your primary ambition is to maximize income from your Second Life existence then focusing your efforts solely upon creating and retailing clothing should be high on your list of potential activities.

Both the required software and excellently detailed templates are available for free, the skills are easily practised and with some discipline, extensive and high quality ranges can be produced. The time involved need not necessarily be extensive. A few hours on most days should be enough to develop a business and an income from Second Life fashion.

Currently there are three commonly employed methods to produce clothing for Second Life.

* The Appearance menu

* Texture maps

* Textured prims.

Of course innovative designers combine two or all three of these techniques to create different and more sophisticated effects.

Using the Appearance menu

Residents can use the Appearance menu to create clothing items. The lengths of the sleeves, collar, etc. can be crudely adjusted along with other features such as how tight the item appears. A colour can be uniformly applied to the item and in addition a texture can be applied as a 'fabric' but this fabric will not be mapped to an avatar's body correctly and the resultant clothing item may well appear to be poorly made. I'm sure you are familiar with this feature and even if you are not then it really doesn't matter because it would be business suicide to make clothes for retail using only this most basic of techniques.

Using Texture maps

To make high quality clothing items that look great on an avatar we need to use a sophisticated graphics program that can:

• Import Adobe Photoshop files.

• Work with layers.

• Manage alpha channels.

The GIMP (www.gimp.org) comes with every function we need to create highly detailed and effective clothing for Second Life and is free to download.

We use templates to create the 2D texture that will be applied to a 3D avatar. These templates have been created to assist us to map the clothing to the avatar and to accurately position details such as buttons, seams and pockets.

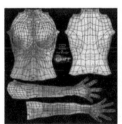 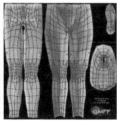 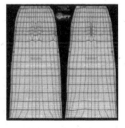

Irie thanks

These wonderfully detailed templates have been produced by Second Life resident Chip Midnight and are currently available from the Download page of the Second Life website. Thank you, Chip Midnight!

We can use these templates to produce textures which we then apply as the 'fabric' to an item of clothing within the Appearance menu. We use the same template to map several different items, for example the shirt, undershirt, upper jacket, upper tattoos and gloves are all produced using the upper body template.

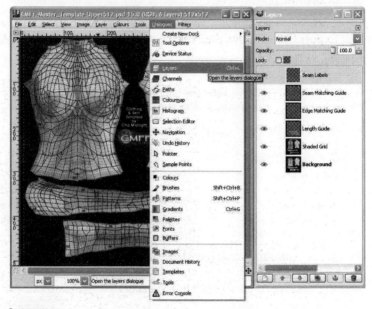

Layers

Download and open the upper body template in GIMP (or similar graphics package) then select **Dialogues > Layers** to open the Layers dialog box (keyboard shortcut **[Ctrl] + [L]**).

Chip's upper body template has six layers each of which we elect to display or hide by clicking on the adjacent 'eye' icon on the Layers dialog box. These layers are only used during the creative process and will be hidden or removed when we create our texture at the end of the process.

Let us first examine how these templates map to an avatar:

1 Open a template using your preferred graphics program (for this example we will open Chip's upper body template in GIMP).

2 Select **File > Save As...** to open the **Save Image** window.

3 From the **Save Image** window, rename the file (e.g. *upper*) then Save in the Desktop folder for convenience.

4 Select **File Type (By Extension)** as TarGa image – click the '+' next to it.

5 Click the **Save** button, then click the **Export** button in the **Export File** window, then the **Save** button in the **Save as TGA** window.

6 From the top menu bar of the viewer select **File > Upload Image (L$10)...** (or use the keyboard shortcut **[Ctrl] + [U]**) and locate the *upper.tga* file. A preview window will open in the viewer, displaying the template texture.

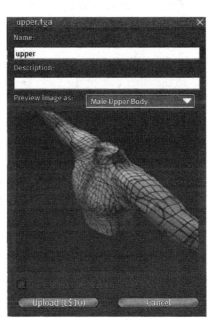

7 Select an **Upper Body** option from the **Preview image as:** drop-down menu. Hold down **[Alt]** and/or **[Ctrl]**, click on the image then drag the mouse to examine the template from various aspects (**[Alt]**) and zoom (**[Ctrl]**) positions.

Irie tip

Throughout the production process, I use this little preview window to regularly check the accuracy and position of clothing details such as joins, seams and edges.

---

8 Assuming everything appears correctly in the preview window click the **Upload (L$10)** button and after a few moments the texture will be displayed within the viewer.

9 Open your inventory ([Ctrl] + [I]). From the top menu of its window select **Create > New Clothes > New Shirt**.

10 Within your inventory, right-click this new shirt and rename 'New Shirt' to 'Upper Template', then right-click again then select **Wear** from the drop-down menu.

11 Right-click on your avatar then select **Appearance** from the pie menu.

12 Select the **Shirt** tab then click on the white **Fabric** panel.

13 Locate the Upper texture (type 'upper' in the filter box of the **Pick: Fabric** window.)

14 Save and close the **Appearance** window.

15 Repeat this procedure with the Lower and/or Skirt templates.

Not the most stylish suit Redgold has ever worn but it does show how the templates map to the body of a Second Life avatar.

Using the Appearance menu to adjust the avatar's size and shape will demonstrate to you just how the 2D templates shift and slide to accurately map around the 3D human form.

Irie note

The left arm is rendered as a mirror image of the right arm so only an avatar's right arm appears in the upper body template. Any text on the sleeve will therefore be reversed on the left arm.

Using templates to create clothing (using GIMP)

I will now take you through the entire process of creating a pair of capri style pants in order to demonstrate how the previously described skills come together to create items of clothing for Second Life.

Open the template

1 Select **File > Open** from the GIMP tool palette.

2 Locate a lower body template file.

3 Click the **Open** button.

The Template file will open in a separate window.

Irie tip

When using GIMP, functions that are available to us can be accessed by right-clicking on the image.

Rename the file

We save a copy so that we don't edit or overwrite our original template file.

1 Right-click the image then select **File > Save As...** from the drop-down menu (or select **File > Save As...** from the image window's menu bar).

2 Rename the new file (e.g jeancapris) then click on the '+' next to **Select File Type (By Extension)** to open a list of file types.

3 Select **GIMP XCF image** then click the **Save** button.

Adding working layers

There are already six layers to this particular template but we will need to add several new working layers on which to paint our capris.

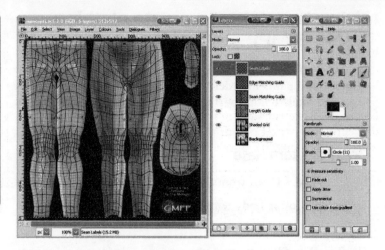

You will quickly discover that using layers makes the task of resizing or positioning clothing details much simpler so don't be shy about adding lots of new layers.

1   From the Layers dialog box ([Ctrl] + [L]) click the **New layer** button. A **New Layer** window will open.

2   Enter '*capri*' as the Layer Name.

3   Select the **Transparency** radio button under **Layer Fill Type**.

4   Click the **OK** button to create the layer.

5   In the **Layers** dialogue box click on the *capri* layer to select it.

6   Use the arrow keys to move the capri layer into a position where the templates can still be used as a guide.

7   Paint the base colour (I usually choose white so I can tint the fabric layer later) and basic shape of the capris onto this layer. Use the templates as a guide.

8   Add the other details such as trim, buttons and pockets as new layers so they may be independently edited, repositioned and/or scaled.

I painted portions of these capris using Gimp features including the paintbrush and pencil. Other details such as the pockets and belt loops I sourced from photos. Some high quality designers refuse to 'photo-source' and exclusively paint their creations; as 'Bikini Queen' Zib Scaggs tells me, 'Photo-realism isn't important to me. My priority is that my clothes look great on Second Life avatars!' Personally I'm happy to use a photo sample of an unidentifiable pocket or cuff to give my creations a hint of real-world authenticity. It's purely a matter of artistic taste.

Irie warning

Photo sampling either entire clothing items or unique/definable design details is not within the 'fair use' of copyright law.

Here I've edited the capris to a point I'm happy with the position of the seams, button, trim, etc. Notice that I have hidden some of the layers (no eye icon). These hidden layers are the layers that were not useful during this particular project.

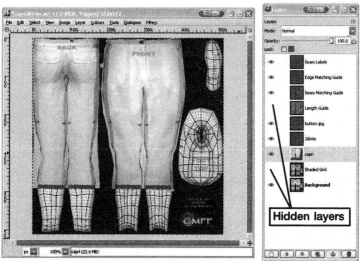

Before we pay to upload the texture into Second Life, it is sensible to see how the capris will appear on an avatar. We do this to check for errors, gaps, seam alignment, etc. Using your preferred search engine you will find free software programs such as *SL Clothes Previewer* created by Johan Durant that allow us to check our creations outside Second Life. Alternatively we can use the upload previewer built into the viewer to the same purpose. Either way we need to convert the image:

1 Hide all the template layers using the eye icons on the Layers dialogue box.

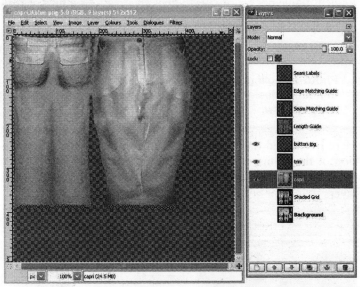

2 Select **File > Save As...** (e.g.) CapriJA

3 Save as either:

   *.png or *.tga for upload pre-view.

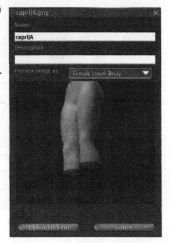

Or

(e.g.) *.jpg for SL Clothes Previewer.

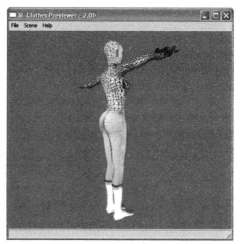

Applying colour

Once we are finished with the design we can then apply colour to our capris. Reverting to the *capriJA.xcf* file we select the 'Capri' layer. In GIMP, the Colorize feature is the easiest way to apply a colour to our layer and in this example I applied a light blue tint to the layer using the slider.

We save this layer as a .png file and once again check it in the Second Life viewer's upload previewer. Once we are happy with our texture we upload the file then create a new pair of pants (**Inventory > Create > New Clothes > New Pants**), wear them and from the Appearance window apply our new texture as the fabric. We then find a willing volunteer to model our new garment and voila!

Of course now is also a perfect time to colourize our creation into other colours such as red, green, yellow, pink, a dark grey, etc. to produce a whole range of capris.

Using prims

More and more clothing is now being designed using increasingly complex prim combinations. Baggy trousers, protruding pockets, belt loops and buckles are all being created as prim objects then worn as attachments. Creating prim clothing is no different from building any other object. Just link a group of prims together into an object, apply some textures, then attach the object to your avatar.

Creating prim hair

Prim hair is one of the most common objects that attach to an avatar and the more stylish residents amongst us own dozens of different 'hairstyles' yet continually remain on the prowl for new and visually effective products to add to their collections. Producing and maintaining a range of high quality and original hair objects can therefore be a lucrative business opportunity.

I produced my own small range of dreadlock style hair over a year ago that continues to outsell all other objects I have made. If I were so inclined, I believe concentrating on hair design, manufacture and retail would maximize my short-term income. Adding to my own range of hair remains high up my 'to do' list and if your ambition is financially motivated I suggest you consider this sector.

My hair is just a collection of prims

Creating effective looking hair is an artistic pursuit (how would that look, would this look better?) rather than a technical exercise (measure, click, snap, click). Producing prim hair is in effect creating an organic-looking sculpture and so a considerable amount of time is spent twisting, curling, styling, prim positioning, staring, examining and prim re-positioning. Unfortunately the building grids and rulers are largely useless during the process though hair is a very satisfying object to build.

There are three elements to creating prim hair:

1 The hair base.

2 The prim hair object.

3 The texture.

Creating the hair base

To prepare an avatar's head we use the Appearance window to create either a bald hair base or style an appropriate hair base to receive our prim hair object:

1 Detach any hair that your avatar is wearing.

2 Select **Create** > **New Body Parts** > **New Hair** from the Inventory menu bar.

3 Right-click the New Hair item (found in the inventory's *Body Parts* folder) then select **Rename** from the drop-down menu. Rename the item to *Hair Base*.

4 Right-click on Hair Base item and select **Wear** from the drop-down menu.

5 Right-click on your avatar then select **Appearance...** from the pie menu.

6 Select the **Hair** tab from the **Appearance** window, then use the Texture panel and the **Color** and **Style** buttons to create your base style. For a bald base reduce the **Hair Volume** slider (under **Style**) to zero.

7 Save and close the Appearance menu when your base is satisfactory (remembering that you can revisit this edit at any time).

Creating the prim hair object

Prim Hair is created by linking variously shaped prims (including flexi-prims) into a wig-type object and is constructed in the same manner as any other prim-based object. Though a tapered tori is the most regularly used prim shape in the construction of prim hair, I would also suggest adjusting and exploring the size, skew, hole size settings and applying various radii and revolutions to tori as well. Also pay a visit to Second Life's leading prim hair retailers to acquire some free demo versions in order to glean what other prim shapes and variations they incorporate into which features of their designs.

Adding flexi prims

Unfortunately we cannot yet add flexible properties to tori so instead we use tapered cylinders and sheet-shaped cubes to produce flexi hair. It is important to experiment with the flexible properties settings to discover the most authentic reaction to movement and/or wind.

Hair texture

Depending on the effect we wish to produce we can either use/ create a completely opaque hair texture or add some transparency and a rough edge to create more effective ends to the hair prims. Learning to create hair textures within your preferred graphics program is both simple and useful.

Irie tip

You don't have to use 'hair' textures for hair. My own hair is made using a compressed gold panel texture! I explored my inventory, experimented and thought it looked best.

Fitting a new prim hair object

1 Locate in your inventory and wear the appropriate hair base item.

2 Locate the new prim hair object in your inventory.

3 From your inventory, right-click the new prim hair object then select **Attach To > Skull**. The new prim hair object will become attached but will be incorrectly oriented.

4 Right-click the attached prim hair then select **Edit** from the object pie menu.

5 Reposition and rotate the hair object using the handles.

Hairstyling is art. How would that look? Does this look better? Experiment, explore, twist, tinker, curl, style, position, stare, adjust, examine from all angles then reposition. Take the time to become a perfectionist.

Prim footwear

With trendy avatars seemingly requiring different shoes and boots for every occasion there are hordes of eager consumers of high quality footwear. Producing and maintaining a range of high quality and original footwear can therefore become a profitable Second Life profession.

There are three components to prim footwear:

* The Second Life shoe.
* The prim shoe object.
* The 'Invisiprim'.

Creating the Second Life shoe

We use the **Appearance** window to create a Second Life shoe, to shape the avatar's feet and platform/heel height to receive our prim footwear objects.

1 Detach any shoes that your avatar is wearing.

2 Select **Create > New Clothes > New Shoes** from the **Inventory** menu bar.

3 Right-click the **New Shoes** item (found in the inventory's *Clothing* folder) then select **Rename** from the drop-down menu. Rename the item, e.g. 'First Shoes'.

4 Right-click on First Shoes item, then select **Wear** from the drop-down menu.

5   Right-click on your avatar, then select **Appearance...** from the pie menu.

6   Select the **Shoes** tab from the **Appearance** window, then use the sliders to create the appropriate foot size, shape and heel.

7   When the Second Life shoe is satisfactory, save and close the **Appearance** menu (remembering that you can revisit this edit when the finished shoe is fitted).

Building prim shoes

Prim footwear is created by linking variously shaped prims in the same manner as any other prim-based object. I've assembled a basic shoe here to explain the fundamentals but they are nothing inspirational. I suggest you visit Second Life's leading footwear retailers to acquire some free demo versions in order to examine their shoes and boots featuring sculpted prims, flexi ribbons and laces, jewels as well as many other stunning details.

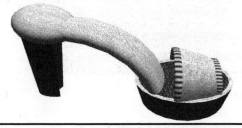

Irie tip

We could just take a copy of the prim shoe to create a left and right version, though I feel it is worth the effort to shape each shoe individually to reflect the shape of the left and right foot. It is this kind of attention to detail that separates the best and most successful manufacturers from the rest.

Applying and adjusting texture

Textures can be used to dramatically enhance the appearance of the footwear. Apply texture to footwear as diligently as you would to any other product.

The Invisiprim

When Second Life shoes (not prim shoes) are worn, the avatar's feet morph a flesh-coloured heel and platform. If prim shoes are then attached, the Second Life shoe's heel and platform are likely to remain hideously visible. An Invisiprim contains a script that makes both the prim and any avatar body part contained within it transparent, and is therefore used to conceal the parts of the Second Life shoe that are not hidden by the prim shoe. You will find various Invisiprim scripts by inputting 'Invisiprim script' into your preferred search engine. Copy and paste the text of an Invisiprim script into a new script then rename it *Invisiprim*.

Create and position an appropriate shaped prim that hides the heel but will not obscure any part of the foot above the insole. I have used a quarter of a stretched cylinder in this example but we may use any prim shape or variation.

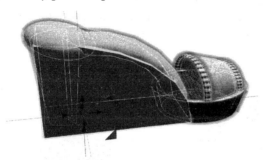

Drop an Invisiprim Script onto the prim object's Contents tab then close the Edit window. Wait a minute and you should see the Invisiprim disappear leaving the prim shoe visible.

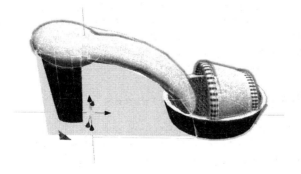

Irie note

Be careful! An Invisiprim script turns the prim not transparent but invisible and therefore we cannot find an Invisiprim using the Highlight transparent view.

Fitting the shoe

1 Locate and wear the appropriate Second Life shoes in your inventory.

2 Locate the right foot new prim shoe object in your inventory.

3 From your inventory, right-click the new prim shoe object then select **Attach To > Right Foot**. The object will become attached but will be incorrectly oriented.

4 Right-click the attached prim shoe then select **Edit** from the object pie menu.

5 Reposition and rotate the shoe using the handles.

6 Mirror these steps to fit the left shoe.

Boots

Each prim boot is typically constructed from two but sometimes three sections; the foot attachment, the lower leg attachment and sometimes an upper leg attachment. Boot creators use a separate attachment for each section in order that the boots stay in position on the legs when an avatar walks.

An example of the amazing footwear leading Second Life retailers are currently producing.

High quality creators provide interest to their shoes and boots using sculpted prims, flexi prims, jewels, straps, decorations and other effects such as scripted walks or bling particle effects.

05 understanding scripting

In this chapter you will learn:

- how to compile and run a script
- how a script operates
- how to write an efficient script

Scripts

Scripts allow Second Life objects to move, listen, talk, operate as a vehicle or weapon, change colour, size or shape and to perform a whole host of other functions.

Linden Scripting Language (**LSL**) is the code used to script the objects we encounter and make in Second Life. A script can be placed inside any in-world object but not inside an avatar. However avatars can and routinely do wear scripted objects such as HUDs, radars, chimeras, bling jewellery, etc.

Compiling and running a script

Scripts can only run from within an object so in order to compile and run a script we must first create a new prim.

1 Create a new prim.

2 Select the **Content** tab from the new prim's **Edit** menu.

3 Click the **New Script** button to create a default script within the object.

4 Close the **Edit** menu.

You will notice the text 'Object: Hello, Avatar!' has been broadcast in open chat. Left-click the object and 'Object: Touched.' is broadcast in chat. Taaaa daaaa! You have just compiled and run an LSL script.

An introduction to scripting

If you already understand how computer programming works then this section can largely be ignored. If scripting is completely new to you then it becomes vital that you understand this simple section before proceeding further.

Grasping the basic principles of scripting proved to be the thorniest branch of my Second Life learning experience. I spent the weekend between Christmas and New Year with my head in the LSL Wiki, digesting article after article and tutorial after tutorial on the subject and for much of the weekend I just didn't get it. Eventually the light came on and my progression towards becoming a proficient scripter at once became rapid. But it is an incredibly simple principle to grasp with the right analogy.

I want to create a useful picture in your imagination...

Imagine a house. It is a very grand house indeed. It is your home (lucky you!). At the front of this house is a large entrance hallway. This entrance hallway is your 'home' or default location and every time you appear, you arrive in this hallway.

In this entrance hallway are two boxes. Written on the first box are the words 'When you arrive, I will say "Hello, Avatar"'. Written on the second box are the words 'If you touch me, then I will say "Touched."'. And basically that is how a script works.

Open the default script, i.e. the one you created in your first scripted object or use **Create > New Script** from the Inventory top menu bar then right-click > Open the 'New Script' created in the inventory *Scripts* folder. Adjust the window as necessary to make the entire script visible and you should see the following:

This default script is our imaginary 'hallway' expressed in LSL.

```
Script: New Script                          _ X
  File    Edit    Help

default
{
    state_entry()
    {
        llSay(0, "Hello, Avatar!");
    }

    touch_start(integer total_number)
    {
        llSay(0, "Touched.");
    }
}




Line 0, Column 0
                                    Save

☑ Running                          Reset
```

In LSL, our imaginary hallway is referred to as a *state* (as is every imaginary room). In this script our hallway is the default state and anything that occurs in our hallway (or default state) is contained between the container (the matched { and }) closest to the left margin. A script must contain a default state as when a script is either started or reset it must start in its default state.

```
Default
{
    ......
}
```

Our two imaginary boxes in the entrance hall are referred to as the script *events*. In the default script these two boxes (or events) are expressed in LSL as:

```
state_entry()
{
    ......
}
```

A **state_entry** event is the first event triggered when the state (imaginary room) is entered.

and...

```
touch_start(integer num_detected)
{
    ......
}
```

A **touch_start** event is triggered when the object is touched.

Anything that might happen when either event is triggered is contained in the subsequent container (matched { and }).

In the default script, a *function* will be called when either event is triggered. These functions are expressed in LSL as:

```
llSay(0, "Hello, Avatar!");
```

This particular function commands the object to say 'Hello, Avatar!' in general chat.

And...

```
llSay(0, "Touched.");
```

This function commands the object to say 'Touched.' in general chat.

Are you with me so far? If so let me create a second useful image in your imagination…

Remember our grand entrance hallway with the two boxes? I hope so. We are now going to change what is written on one of the boxes in our hallway. The first box still reads 'When you arrive, I will say "Hello, Avatar!"'. But now written on the second box are the words 'If you touch me, firstly I will say "Sending you to the kitchen" then I will transport you directly to the kitchen.'

Let us imagine we touch this 'new' second box. The box obediently says 'Sending you to the kitchen' and we are then magically transported to our kitchen.

Arriving in the kitchen we hear the words 'Welcome to the kitchen Avatar!' and discover two new boxes. On the first box are written the words 'When you arrive, I will say "Welcome to the kitchen Avatar!"' (Ah! This explains the state entry message we just heard.) On the second box are written the words 'If you touch me I will firstly say "Sending you to the hallway" then I will transport you directly back to the hallway.'

Let us imagine we touch this second box. The box obediently says "Sending you to the hallway" and then we are magically transported back to the hallway. When we arrive in the hallway, of course, the first box in the hallway notices our entry and says "Hello, Avatar!".

The following is our current imagining expressed in LSL.

```
Default
{
  state_entry()
  {
    llSay(0, "Hello, Avatar!");
  }

  touch_start(integer num_detected)
  {
    llSay(0, "Sending you to the kitchen");
    state kitchen;
  }
}
```

```
state kitchen
{
  state_entry()
  {
    llSay(0, "Welcome to the kitchen Avatar!");
  }
  touch_start(integer num_detected)
  {
    llSay(0, "Sending you to the hallway");
    state default;
  }
}
```

The significant difference between this script and the default script is that within this second script there are two states; the default state (imaginary hallway) and the kitchen state.

Let us first examine the contents of the default state (contained within the first container (closest to the left margin).

The first event is the **state_entry** event and is identical to the **state_entry** event in the default script.

The second event is a **touch_start** event and contains the following two functions:

```
llSay(0, "Sending you to the kitchen");
```

This commands our object to say 'Sending you to the kitchen'.

```
state kitchen;
```

This function calls our script to change state to 'kitchen'.

Irie note

Logic dictates that in our imaginary home we can only exist in one room at any one time and as such a script can only be in one state at any one time. Our script can be in **either** the default state **or** the kitchen state. The script can move between states but the script cannot be in both states.

Examine the 'kitchen' state now. Pretty simple isn't it? If not then start reading this chapter again.

Exactly copy this *kitchen* script into a new script and click the **Save** button. You should see the message 'Compile successful, saving...' appear in the box below the script editing area. After a short pause you should see the message 'Save complete' appear there. If you received any error messages when saving or running a script, check and double-check for accuracy. It is most likely that you have omitted or added a curly bracket or missed a semicolon at the end of a function call. Brackets, parentheses, and semicolons must all be perfectly in place before a script will run.

Find the script in your inventory (it's probably still called 'New Script', right-click it and select **Rename**. Rename it something appropriate like 'kitchen script' then drag the script into the contents tab of a new prim or alternatively onto the object itself whilst holding down [**Ctrl**].

"Hello, Avatar!". Now touch the box. And again. And again!

The script of course is not a big imaginary house but instead is contained within this object. What is actually happening is:

1 The new script enters default state and
   a. Calls the function in **state_entry**
   b. The object says 'Hello, Avatar!'

2 The object waits to be touched.

3 When touched the script calls the functions in the **touch_start** event:
   a. The object says 'Sending you to the kitchen'
   b. The script enters kitchen state.

4 The script calls the function in the '**state_entry**' event:
   a. The object says 'Welcome to the kitchen Avatar!'

5 The object waits to be touched.

6 When touched the script calls the functions in the **touch_start** event:
   a. The object says 'Sending you to the hallway'.
   b. The script enters default state.

7 ... and the whole process starts again.

Important things to know about scripting

Nesting

A nested container is one included within another. Indenting nested containers is not required for a script to run correctly but is commonly accepted as good practice as indenting the contents of each nested container by a further tab does make a script a lot easier to comprehend.

```
{
    {
        .....
    }
}
```

Comments

A comment is most often used to help scripters explain a line of code or section of script or to temporarily obscure a line of code from the compiler (the software which changes our script into code the computer can understand). Comments are defined on a single line by using '//'. Every word to the right of '//' is considered a comment and will be ignored by the script compiler.

```
//this is a comment
//and will be ignored by the script compiler

Default //this is the state
{
  state_entry() //this is an event
  {
    llSay(0, "Hello, Avatar!"); //this is a
function
    //llSay(0, "Goodbye, Avatar!"); (this line is
commented out)
```

LSL states

A state is a section of the script that, when active, is waiting for at least one event.

* Only one state can be active at any one time.

- All scripts must have a default state with at least one event in it (many scripts *only* contain a default state).

- With the exception of the default, states can be freely named. A state is defined by the word **state** followed by its name.

- The contents of a state are enclosed between two curly brackets (its container).

LSL events

Events are contained within states and are either triggered by actions happening to or around the object the script resides in or alternatively triggered from within the script itself. Events run one at a time and in the order they are triggered. Once triggered the event calls the functions held within its container one at a time and in the order they are written.

We've already come across the state_entry event (triggered by the state being entered) and the touch_start event (triggered when an avatar touches an object). Unlike a state, an event cannot be freely named.

All LSL events with their trigger definitions can be found listed within the Second Life LSL Portal: **http://wiki.secondlife.com/wiki/LSL_Portal**

LSL functions

When an event is triggered then the functions held within that event's containers will be called one at a time and in their scripted order. Functions can either be user-defined or built-in. Those built into LSL all start with two lowercase Ls. We have already used the built-in function **llSay()** which commanded our object to speak. All LSL functions with their definitions and examples uses can be found listed within the Second Life LSL Portal: **http://wiki.secondlife.com/wiki/LSL_Portal**

Functions take information from the brackets () that follow them. When we position the cursor over a function in the script window, a pop-up will be displayed that tells us of what information the function is expecting and a brief description of the function performed.

```
llSay(0, "Touched.");
```

```
llSay(integer channel, string msg)
says msg on channel
```

The **llSay** function displays a pop-up that informs us that it expects two values of a specific data type; an *integer* (i.e. a whole number) to identify the channel on which the message will be broadcast and a *string* (i.e. the string of words and/or characters to broadcast). The llSay function will not accept other values.

In the example above we see the integer value is '0' (the channel for general chat) and the string value is 'Hello, Avatar!'. The result is that when this Function is called then 'Hello, Avatar!' will be broadcast on the general chat channel zero, i.e. 'says msg on channel'.

LSL data types

Integer: In LSL a valid integer value is any whole number between –2147483648 and +2147483647. Example integer values:

```
1, 5, 57, 609846
```

Float: In LSL a valid float value is any number (with or without decimals) between 1.175494351E-38 and +3.402823466E+38. Example float values:

```
1.2, 3.0, 5.97, 9.34593
```

String: In LSL a string value contains a sequence of characters. Any character may be used in a string. In LSL string values are enclosed in double quotes. Example string values:

```
"Irie Tsure"
"1234565abcdef!"£$%^"
"Hello Avatar!"
```

Key: A key is another name for the unique identifier (UUID) of every item, object and resident in Second Life. In LSL key values are enclosed in quotes. Example key value:

```
"c541c47f-e0c0-058b-ad1a-d6ae3a4584d9"
```

Vector: In LSL, a vector value is used to define a position, a speed and direction or a colour.

- Position: x, y and z expressed in metres.
- Velocity: x, y and z expressed in m/s.
- Colour: x = red, y = green, z = blue.

A valid vector value contains three float values separated by commas and enclosed by < and >. Example vector value:

```
<1.00, 2.00, 3.00>
```

Rotation: In LSL a rotation value is used to define an object's orientation. A valid value contains four float values separated by commas and enclosed by < and >. Example rotation value:

```
<1.00, 2.00, 3.00, 1.00 >
```

List: A list contains a series of other valid data values separated by commas and enclosed by [and]. Example list values:

```
[0, 1, 2, 3, 4, 5]
["Caleb", "Charlton", "Elis", "Alf"]
[6, 3.141592654, "Random", < 1.0, 2.0, 3.0 >]
```

LSL constants

Constants are values that never change and are used to simplify code. Example constants:

```
PI
```

always produces a float value of:

3.14159265358979323846264338327950

```
PUBLIC_CHANNEL
```

is always channel 0

```
NULL_KEY
```

always indicates an empty key value

```
ZERO_ROTATION
```

always produces a rotation value of <0.0, 0.0, 0.0, 1.0>

All LSL constants along with their definitions can be found listed in the Second Life LSL Portal: **http://wiki.secondlife.com/wiki/ LSL_Portal**

LSL flow statements

Within a script flow statements such as **if, else, do,** etc. control which code is run and when code is run. Let me create a picture in your imagination. It is so much easier.

I hope you remember our hallway and our boxes. Imagine that the first box now has written on it: 'If the owner of this box touches this box then I will say "Hello Boss!" otherwise I will say "Hello Avatar!"'. This would be expressed in LSL using flow statements as follows:

```
default
{
 touch_start(integer num_detected)
 {
  if (llDetectedKey(0) == llGetOwner())
  llSay(0, "Hello Boss!");
  else
  llSay(0, "Hello Avatar!");
 }
}
```

And broken down it works like this:

```
1.
 touch_start(integer num_detected)
```

When I am touched...

```
2.
if (llDetectedKey(0) == llGetOwner())
 llSay(0, "Hello Boss!");
```

Detect the avatar and detect the object owner (two separate LSL Functions) and **if** they are identical then say 'Hello Boss!' on chat channel zero.

```
3.
 else
 llSay(0, "Hello Avatar!");
```

Otherwise say 'Hello Avatar!' on chat channel zero.

All LSL flow statements with their definitions and examples of usage can be found listed within the Second Life LSL Portal: **http://wiki.secondlife.com/wiki/LSL_Portal**

Declaring variables

A variable is a snippet of code in a script where we store a value (i.e. a string, integer, float, vector, rotation, key, or list) in order that this information can be accessed more than once and from elsewhere in the script.

For example, within a script we can command that the text 'gOwner' should be considered a *key* by declaring the variable globally: A *global variable* is declared before the default state (therefore will apply to all states), is customarily prefaced with a 'g' and is accessible from anywhere in the script.

```
key gOwner;

default
```

A *local variable* is declared and accessible only within the scope of a container (i.e. between a matched { and } including any further nested containers).

```
key gOwner;
default
{
 gOwner = llGetOwner();
 touch_start(integer num_detected)
 {
  if (llDetectedKey(0) == gOwner)
  {
   llSay(0, "Hello Boss!");
  }
 }
}
```

We use variables to simplify and speed up the process of running a script. Let me create yet another picture in your imagination…

In our entrance hallway are two boxes. Written on the first box are the words 'When anyone arrives, I will say "Hello Avatar!"'. Written on the second box are the words "*If* the owner of this box touches this box *then* I will say "Hello Boss!" then I will say "Sending you to the kitchen" then I will transport you directly to the kitchen *otherwise* (i.e. any other avatar) I will say "Hello Avatar!".'

Plate 1: There are opportunities in the fashion industry

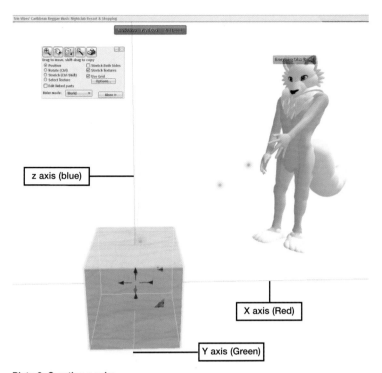

Plate 2: Creating a prim

Plate 3: Sculpted fruit by Qarl Linden

Plate 4: Hair styles can also provide an income

```
key gOwner;
default
{
    state_entry()
    {
        llSay(0, "Hello, Avatar!");
    }

    touch_start(integer num_detected)
    {
    gOwner = llGetOwner();
        if (llDetectedKey(0) == gOwner)
        {
            llSay(0, "Hello Boss!");
            llSay(0, "Sending you to the kitchen");
            state kitchen;
        }
        else
            llSay(0, "Hello Avatar!");
    }
}

state kitchen
{
    state_entry()
    {
        llSay(0, "Welcome to the kitchen Avatar!");
    }

    touch_start(integer num_detected)
    {
        gOwner = llGetOwner();
        if (llDetectedKey(0) == gOwner)
        {
            llSay(0, "Hello Boss!");
            llSay(0, "Sending you to the hallway.");
            state default;
        }
        else
        {
            llSay(0, "Are you lost?");
            state default;
        }
    }
}
```

Plate 5: Colour makes scripts easier to follow

Plate 6: A good advertisement will help to create your brand identity

Plate 7: Accessibility is important in a retail venue

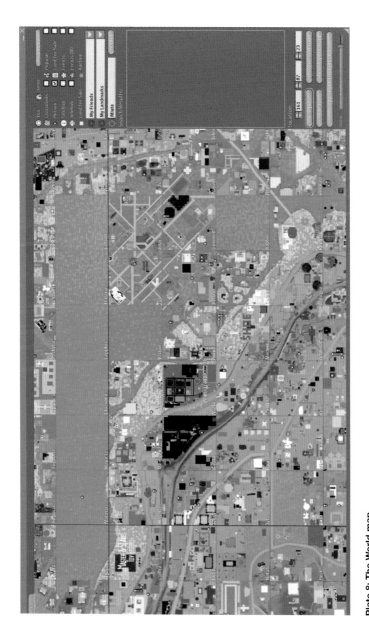

Plate 8: The World map

Plate 9: The ITunes store – real-world sales in Second Life

Let us imagine we (as the owner) touch this 'new' second box. The box obediently says 'Hello Boss!' then says 'Sending you to the kitchen' and then we are magically transported to our kitchen.

Arriving in the kitchen we hear the words 'Welcome to the kitchen Avatar!' spoken and discover two new boxes. On the first box are written the words 'When you arrive, I will say "Welcome to the kitchen Avatar!".' On the second box are written the words ''If the owner of this box touches this box then I will say "Hello Boss!" then I will say "Sending you to the hallway" then I will transport you directly to the hallway *otherwise* I will say "Are you lost?"'.

Let us imagine we touch this second box. The box obediently says 'Hello Boss!' then says 'Sending you to the hallway' and then we are magically transported back to the hallway. When we arrive in the hallway, of course, the first box in the hallway notices our entry and says "Hello Boss!'.

When we put these two states together into a working script, we should look to simplify the script using variables and might end up with something like the one shown on page 86.

Irie note

I hope you noticed that in our example kitchen script it is impossible for any avatar but the owner to change the script state to 'kitchen' and therefore much of the flow control within the kitchen state is redundant and is included only for the purpose of example.

The built-in LSL script editor (compiler) very kindly changes the colour of any text that it recognizes, using these colour codes.

- ◆ Maroon   States and functions
- ◆ Light blue   Events
- ◆ Blue   Flow controls (if, for, while, etc.)
- ◆ Dark blue   Constants
- ◆ Semi-light green   Type declarations (integer, string, etc.)
- ◆ Dark/pale green   Strings
- ◆ Orange   Comments

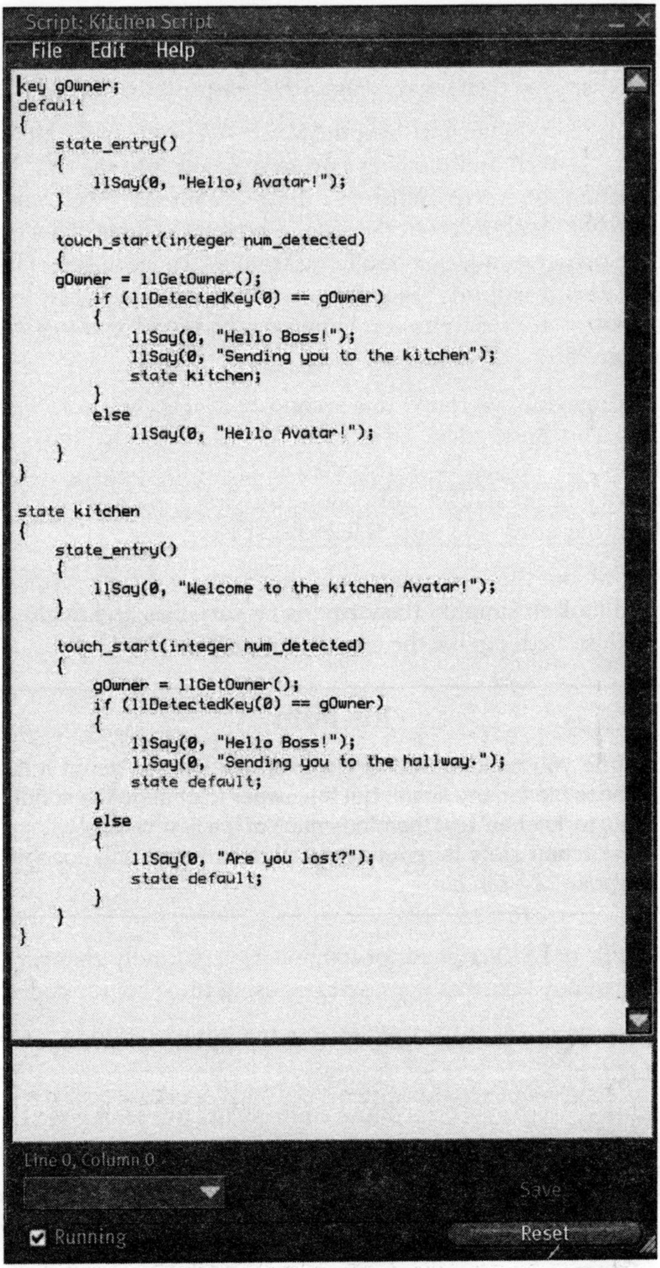

Script: Kitchen Script   — ×

File   Edit   Help

```
key gOwner;
default
{
    state_entry()
    {
        llSay(0, "Hello, Avatar!");
    }

    touch_start(integer num_detected)
    {
    gOwner = llGetOwner();
        if (llDetectedKey(0) == gOwner)
        {
            llSay(0, "Hello Boss!");
            llSay(0, "Sending you to the kitchen");
            state kitchen;
        }
        else
            llSay(0, "Hello Avatar!");
    }
}

state kitchen
{
    state_entry()
    {
        llSay(0, "Welcome to the kitchen Avatar!");
    }

    touch_start(integer num_detected)
    {
        gOwner = llGetOwner();
        if (llDetectedKey(0) == gOwner)
        {
            llSay(0, "Hello Boss!");
            llSay(0, "Sending you to the hallway.");
            state default;
        }
        else
        {
            llSay(0, "Are you lost?");
            state default;
        }
    }
}
```

Line 0, Column 0

▼   Save

☑ Running   Reset

I hope this chapter has offered a simple introduction and a clear overview of how LSL operates but please don't be fooled; most of your scripting learning is yet to come. The LSL Portal (Wiki) partners all scripters on most scripting projects as the continuous source of the information we need to make our scripts work. But you should now have the framework of understanding into which to set these elements.

The LSL Portal (**wiki.secondlife.com/wiki/LSL_Portal**) is a ready resource for scripting solutions as well as discussing, featuring and previewing the latest developments and thinking around LSL.

Debugging

There are plenty of errors that can prevent a script from running properly or from running at all. Problems within a script are referred to as *bugs* or *glitches* and it is attention to the details that is usually the cure.

The most common signal that a script is not compiling properly is when we try to save the script an error message is displayed within the Script window:

```
Script: New Script                              _ ×
  File    Edit    Help
default
{
    state_entry()
    {
        llSay(0, "Hello, Avatar!")
    }

    touch_start(integer total_number)
    {
        llSay(0, "Touched.");
    }
}
```

```
(5, 4) : ERROR : Syntax error
```

Line 5, Column 4

Save

☑ Running   Reset

The compiler's message displays the error type and its location within the script (line 5, character 4). In this example, I have carelessly omitted the required semi-colon that should be positioned at the end of the llSay function within the state entry event and this omission prevented the script from compiling.

How to write a script the Irie way

1 **Make the script work.** The most important aspect of a script is that it functions properly and does what we want it to do.

2 **Make the code neat and readable.** Once the script works ensure that the code is properly indented and appropriately commented.

3 **Optimize the code.** Examine the script with a view to simplification, for example by declaring variables.

Irie note

There are several example scripts in the Library section of your inventory.

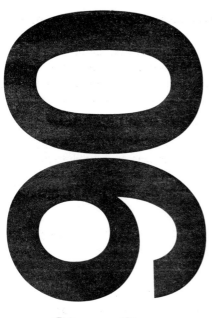

06

creating animations

In this chapter you will learn:

- how Second Life animations work

- how to make an animation

- how to upload an animation into Second Life

An introduction to animating

An animation is a file containing a set of instructions that causes an avatar to engage in a sequence of movements. Creating animations is a simple skill to learn; the tricky bit is producing great looking animations and that comes with practice and industry.

QAvimator (www.qavimator.org) is the freely downloadable software package that I use to produce BVH animation files for Second Life. The BVH file contains the information that describes each body part's rotation and position along a timeline.

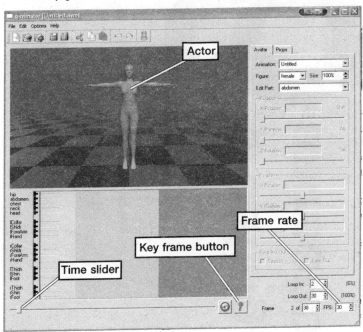

QAvimator camera controls

To **rotate** the camera around the actor we click on the floor then hold down the button. When we then move the mouse horizontally (left and right) or vertically (towards and away from you), the camera's view will rotate accordingly around the actor.

To **zoom** the camera's view towards or away from the actor we click on the floor then hold down [**Alt**] and the mouse button.

When we then move the mouse vertically, the camera's view will zoom in and out from the actor.

To **pan** the camera's view around the stage we click on the floor then hold down [**Shift**] and the button. When we then move the mouse horizontally or vertically, the camera's view will pan to reflect this movement.

Animation Speed

The default speed of QAvimator animation is 30 frames per second (FPS) and therefore a three-second animation will require 90 frames. Luckily we do not need to animate 90 individual frames. For example and depending upon the level of control we require over the animation, we might only animate every fifth, tenth or even thirtieth frame and let QAvimator work out what should happen between these 'keyframes' (interpolate).

Creating animations using QAvimator

The QAvimator's default avatar (referred to as the 'actor') is female but if you would prefer to work with a male actor then select male from the **Figure** drop-down menu.

Getting started

How long will the animation last? Second Life lets us upload animations of a maximum duration of 30 seconds. To make ours last three seconds, we change the number of frames to 90.

The first frame

The first frame of an animation is used by the viewer as the animation's reference point to position the avatar relative to the Second Life grid and is not shown in-world. A Second Life static pose therefore comprises of two separate frames; the reference frame (frame 1) and the actual pose (frame 2).

The first pose

We now have 90 frames ready for our use but must ignore the first frame as it only acts as a reference.

1 Move the animation to the second frame by moving the timeline slider.

2 Click the key-frame button to indicate that frame 2 is our first keyframe.

3 Select the body part we want to move first from the **Edit Part:** drop-down menu or by left-clicking the relative body part on the actor.

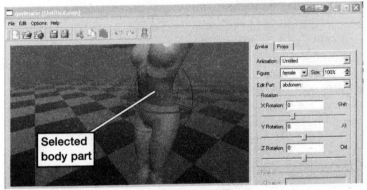

Selected body part

For example clicking on the actor's abdomen (or selecting 'abdomen' from the Edit Part drop-down menu) highlights the actor's abdomen in red and displays the abdomen's X, Y, and Z rotational axes. The X Rotation, Y Rotation and Z Rotation input fields and sliders are used to rotate this selected body part.

Alternatively, when we left-click on a body part and hold down [Ctrl], the blue circle indicating the Z axis will thicken and the mouse can be used to move the selected part in the same manner as when using the Z Rotation slider. [Shift] and [Alt] perform the same function with the X and Y axes respectively.

To move two matched limbs at the same time and by the same degree, we hold down [Shift] then double-click either of the matched limbs we wish to move. The selected matched limbs will be highlighted in yellow and can be moved together using the controls previously described.

The hip

When we click on the actor's hip (or select **Hip** from **Edit Part:** menu) three more active **Position** sliders are displayed. Adjusting these sliders moves the actor around the stage. This is because the hip functions differently from other body parts in so much as it acts as the positional reference point for the animation, i.e. when we want it to move around vertically or horizontally (e.g. for walking, dancing or jumping) it is the hip body part that we reposition and the actor is repositioned accordingly.

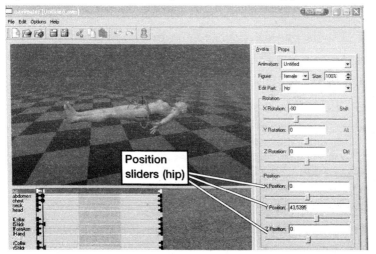

When selected, the hip body part also acts to control the actor's body aspect and therefore adjusting the Rotation slider X axis to −90° will cause the actor to recline around the X axis (as above). Similarly adjusting the hip body part Y and Z Rotation sliders also serves to rotate the actor around the relevant axis.

Irie tip

Take enough time here to explore and familiarize yourself with the QAvimator camera and positioning controls.

---

1 Within the first key-frame (i.e. frame 2) adjust the actor's body parts into the initial pose or starting position of your animation.

2 Use the timeline slider to move to frame 30.

3 Adjust the actor's body parts into the secondary position of your animation.

4 Once finished, click the Key-frame button to indicate that frame 30 is a priority animation frame.

5 Use the timeline slider to move to frame 60.

6 Adjust the body parts into the third position of the animation.

7 Once finished, click the Key-frame button to indicate that frame 60 is a priority animation frame.

8 Use the timeline slider to move back to frame 2.

9 Select **Edit > Copy** from the QAvimator menu bar.

10 Use the timeline slider to move to frame 90.

11 Select **Edit > Paste** from the QAvimator menu bar.

> We make the first and last key-frames identical in order that our animation will loop seamlessly.

12 Click the Key-frame button to indicate that frame 90 is a priority animation frame.

13 Click the **Play** button and check the animation for errors.

14 Once we are happy with the finished animation we name then save the animation file as a *.BVH file (**File > Save as...** from the QAvimator menu bar).

Uploading an animation

To upload an animation into Second Life:

1 Select **File > Upload Animation (L$10)...** from the Second Life viewer's top menu bar.

2 Select the animation file you wish to upload then click **Open**.

3 Edit the relevant options in the displayed animation upload window (see below).

4 Preview and check the animation in the displayed animation upload window.

5 Press **Upload (L$10)** to upload the animation.

Irie's animating tips

* QAvimator provides a useful feature that restricts the movements of the actor's body parts to limits of natural extension. We activate this 'Joint Limits' feature from the QAvimator menu bar (**Options** > then tick **Joint Limits**).

* Don't adjust all the body parts at every keyframe. Work on each single body part throughout the full duration of the animation then return and work with the next body part.

* Adjust the legs then feet last as you will need to make them appear correctly orientated and positioned relative to the ground.

* Indentify errors quickly by playing the developing animation regularly and examining the actor from several angles.

* It is crucial that the animation is working properly before uploading it into Second Life. If the animation is not performing properly then it is very unlikely to play in-world and you will waste L$10.

The Animation Upload window

The animation upload window provides text fields, value fields and menus that affect how the animation will play in-world as well as a preview feature.

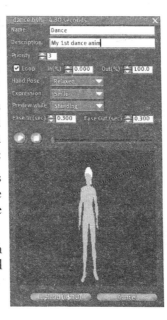

Displayed in the upload window's title bar are both the filename and the animation's duration. Within the window are the following fields:

Name: The editable field displays the name the animation will be given when it is uploaded into the inventory.

Description: This field is for when we want to record some additional helpful or explanatory text.

Priority: Animation priorities range in whole number values from 0 to 4. An animation with a priority value of 0 will not be played when any other animations are playing but an animation with a priority value of 4 will override any other playing animation of a lower priority.

Setting a high priority value to your own animations reduces the risk of them being overridden in-world by other animations.

Loop: Ticking the Loop checkbox determines that the animation will replay repeatedly once it is triggered in-world. Two frame static poses must be looped in order to remain posed.

In(%) and Out(%): These values are used to dictate where the animation will start (default 0%) and end (default 100%). For example if either the 'In(%)' value or the 'Out(%)' value is set to 50.0 then the animation would either start from or stop precisely halfway through the animation.

Hand Pose: This drop-down menu lists the potential hand poses that can be applied to your animation. The selected pose will not be displayed on the avatar in the preview panel.

Expression: This drop-down menu lists the potential facial expressions that can be applied to the avatar whilst the animation is playing in-world. The selected expression will not be displayed on the avatar in the preview panel.

Preview while: Selecting an option from this drop-down menu changes the posture of the avatar in the preview window. You can preview the animation while **Standing, Walking, Sitting,** or **Flying.**

Ease In (sec) and Ease Out (sec): These fields dictate the time allowed for an avatar to interpolate into the animation from his or her current pose.

Previewing the Animation

We preview the animation by clicking the **Play/Pause** and **Stop** buttons above the preview panel. This offers us a final opportunity to check the file is playing correctly before we spend our hard-earned Linden dollars on the upload. Hold down **[Alt]** and/or **[Ctrl]**, click on the preview panel then drag the mouse to examine the animation from various aspects ([**Alt**]) and zoom ([**Ctrl**]) positions.

Irie tip

If the animation does not look right or run correctly within the preview panel then it is almost certain that if you upload the animation into Second Life it will not perform as you hope. Click Cancel, re-edit the animation then try again.

The uploaded animation will be found within the **Inventory > Animations** system folder. All the animations contained here can be activated by double-clicking the animation name.

Activating the animation displays an animation dialog box displaying a **Play in World** and a **Play Locally** button. Clicking Play Locally allows us to preview the animation in-world without it appearing to other residents. Clicking Play in World triggers the animation normally and for all to see.

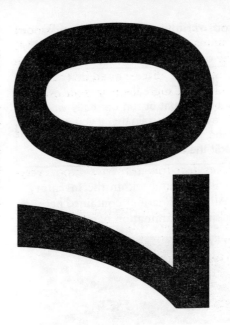

07 putting it all together

In this chapter you will learn:

- how to engender inspiration and design ideas
- how building, texturing and scripting come together
- my step-by-step approach to the creative process

So we now have all our creative skills at our fingertips. We can build, texture, script and animate. It wasn't so hard was it? Of course we are all still at the outset of our Second Life existence and as such still have much to learn, discover and invent. Time, knowledge and practice will be the ingredients in your own entrepreneurial success... so crack on!

'But what shall I build dear Irie, dear Irie?' Well anything, dear Reader.

'But where will I get my ideas dear Irie, dear Irie?' From everywhere, dear Reader!

An uncomplicated strategy to spawn the creative process is to build high quality items as we require them. You want a new anything? Don't go shopping but build it. A new outfit? Then get busy with your preferred graphics program.

The creative process

I try to apply one of two basic principles to my Second Life creativity. The item must either be a design new to Second Life or a significant improvement over an existing design within it. To me there is absolutely no merit in copying an existing item or worse, making an inferior impression of something that already exists here.

Our DJ Manager Redgold Greene (cool name) and I were never much impressed with the DJ turntables found in most Second Life nightclubs. The turntables we'd seen elsewhere are two prim representations with the turntable platter perpetually rotating. I'll quickly make such an example:

1 Using GIMP we create a couple of textures that will not entangle us in any copyright issues.

2 I search Google Images using the term 'DJ Turntable'.

3 I find a couple of appropriate images, right-click on these images then save them to my desktop for simple location.

4 I open them in GIMP and edit any copyright issues from the images by making them unidentifiable.

5   A slightly tapered cylinder provides the platter on the cube base.

6   Applying the textures to the top surfaces produces our basic turntable.

7   A rotation script is dropped into the turntable platter.

A 2-prim turntable may be perfect for your own 'low-prim' environment but it is unlikely to generate much interest in the marketplace.

How can we improve it?

Redgold and I agreed that we would compromise with 'prim-efficiency' to create a more eye-catching turntable. We also decided to add some unique features.

◆   The tone arm and other aspects of the turntable, unlike the basic turntable, will not be included in the texture but created separately using prims for a more authentic appearance.

◆   The textures will be of higher quality and more accurately represent all sides of a turntable.

◆   The LED and strobe lights will produce tiny amounts of light and 'glow'.

◆   A realistic reflection will be included on the record surface.

◆   The turntable platter will be touch start, touch stop and include a timeout feature.

◆   When touched the tone arm will drop onto the record then travel slowly across the surface. Once the record is 'played' it will rise then return more quickly to its rest.

...And so to production. Redgold Greene created the turntable and arm (very beautifully I think) and I tried to get my head around solving the scripting challenges posed by the features we wished to include.

> ### Irie tip
>
> Widening and practising the range of your building, texturing and scripting skills broadens your 'creative vocabulary' and therefore you will form more elegant solutions to your creative challenges.

The challenges

1 The build

Time is the only solution to a high quality build. Redgold Greene spent the necessary hours experimenting with textures and prims to create a very realistic looking turntable and tone arm.

2 The reflection

Our basic turntable does not have a reflection edited onto its surface texture because as the platter rotates, any reflection painted onto the record surface would rotate with the record in a wholly unrealistic manner.

To add realism we added a small degree of transparency to the record surface then placed a 'reflection' prim slightly beneath the surface of the record prim. The 'reflection prim' remains static when the record rotates. Our DJ turntable is intended to be placed in a nightclub environment so we also added a random colour change script to the reflection prim to make the reflection change colour every few seconds for added dancehall authenticity.

3 Touch Start/Stop

A simple two-state rotation script is created (see below) and dropped into the platter prim.

```
default
{
   state_entry()
   {
       llTargetOmega(<0,0,0>,-PI,1.0);
   }
   on_rez(integer start_param)
   {
       llTargetOmega(<0,0,0>,-PI,1.0);
   }
   touch_start(integer num_detected)
   {
       state spinning;
   }
}

state spinning
{
   state_entry()
   {
       llTargetOmega(<0,0,1>,-PI,1.0);
       llSetTimerEvent(1600)
   }
   touch_start(integer num_detected)
   {
       llResetScript();
   }
   timer()
   {
       llResetScript();
   }
   on_rez(integer start_param)
   {
       state default;
   }
}
```

The default state's *touch_start* event changes the script state from the default state (i.e. not spinning) to the spinning state.

Within the spinning state, the *touch_start* event, the *timer* event and the *on_rez* event all return the script to the default (non-spinning) state.

4 Tone arm

'There is more than one way to skin a cat!' Please bear in mind that I'm also still learning and the solutions I stumbled upon are certainly not the only way to provide the functionality we wanted and probably not the most elegant. But these solutions work and that is the main thing!

When touched, we wanted the tone arm to start drifting gradually across the record surface towards the centre, then lift, then return more quickly to the resting (default) position. To create this functionality we initially separated the tone arm and the rest of our turntable into two distinct objects.

You should already know this!

1 Select the object to divide (e.g. turntable).

2 [Ctrl] + [Shift] + [L] (unlink).

3 [Shift] + **left click** the prims to unselect (e.g. tone arm prims).

4 [Ctrl] + [L] (link).

5 Select the tone arm prims.

6 [Ctrl] + [L] (link).

Tone-arm script placed in this 'axis' prim

Scripting the tone arm (as with most things in Second Life) was fairly simple; adjusting the script to create just the right amount of rotation was the time-consuming aspect of the process.

I scripted the tone arm object (within the touch_start event) to first check its orientation (using a **llGetPos** function) then rotate a fraction of a turn (using a **llSetRot** function). I then repeatedly called the set rotation function until the needle reached the centre of the record. I experimented and adjusted the variables in both the degree of rotation and the number of repeats to create authentic paced travel. I repeated this process to return the tone arm to rest but used larger degrees of rotation combined with fewer increments in order to create the effect of a quicker return of the tone arm towards its resting position. The lift and drop of the tone arm was produced using the same method but by applying the tiny degree of required rotation to the vertical axis.

I'm not the world's most practised mathematician so it was more practical for me to use experimentation within variables rather than employ some kind of mathematical formula to calculate the most appropriate increments.

Once I was satisfied that the tone arm moved authentically, I dropped a copy of it into the **Contents** tab of the turntable object along with a script that functions to render the tone arm in the correct position when the turntable is rendered in-world. The position the tone arm is rendered, was again sought using experimentation within the position and rotation variables of the **llRezObject** function.

I did not discover a solution to the issue that the tone arm renders in a position relative to the turntable object but at a rotation relative to the sim. The result is that it is essential to ensure the root prim of the turntable is orientated to 0,0,0 in order to render the tone arm in the correct position. Of course if the tone arm renders incorrectly then it can be repositioned easily and as required, but that is not elegant.

Our finished product is 23 prims in total and therefore becomes a touch unpalatable for low prim environments. But our priority was to produce a high quality turntable and prim-efficiency was never an issue for this particular build. The result of our labours is not only a high quality object that suits our own purposes but also a unique product that we can retail should we wish to.

Growth and further income could be generated from our project:

* By creating turntables in different colours and styles.

* By creating a low prim version.

* By creating a DJ animation for an accompanying pose-ball.

* By creating accompanying high quality DJ equipment.

* By creating accompanying high quality nightclub equipment.

Irie tips for inspiration

Trying to figure out what products to build and in what style should present few hurdles for the imaginative.

1 Build the objects, items and clothing you need as you require them.

2 Consider and notice real-world objects and solutions that might transfer well into the Second Life environment.

3 When considering a new product, browse the Internet for examples of various designs and innovations.

4 Examine other builders' Second Life creations to incorporate good ideas into your own work and to discover where existing designs may be improved.

5 Play and experiment with prims and their features for more of those 'WOW! That would make a great (insert your own product here)!' moments.

6 Keep learning! Regularly reading both the Second Life and LSL Wikis will keep you abreast with the latest thinking, solutions, features, functions and discoveries.

08

retail outlets and venues

In this chapter you will learn:

- what to look for in your first store or venue
- practical solutions to selling
- how to broadcast music across your parcel
- how to minimize lag in your area
- how to grow your business

There are thousands of Second Life retailers selling an unimaginable array of goods. Once you have created a few high quality products, especially once other residents show some interest in your creations then it is not unusual to start exploring the idea of acquiring some retail space of your own.

Start small

One of the fastest routes to failure is to prejudge the largely undefined marketplace that is Second Life. We may love our own products and concepts (I always do), our friends may admire our creativity, our plans may be grand, but when assessed as a viable business project then the Second Life marketplace becomes the only significant judge.

Do not be tempted to invest in a huge space. Do not buy half a sim or even worse a whole one in order to test a theory. Land in Second Life is not cheap and your income will almost certainly fall horribly short of your costs. The key to in-world entrepreneurial success is to cover your costs and in order to do that you will need to grow organically from a small but relatively risk-free base.

To rent or to buy space?

Land that can be used for retail activity is available for purchase or rental on the Mainland and also from residents on their own private estates. To buy land on the Mainland residents require a Premium Second Life account. This is not required to rent space from other residents or to purchase Private Estate land.

I bought my first parcel on the Mainland back in the days of the highly discounted and now abandoned First Land scheme (and sharply rising land prices). But if I arrived in Second Life today then I would almost certainly look to rent a store in a busy shopping mall to get my foot on the first rung of the retailing ladder. Renting in a shopping mall offers you the benefits that you will not need to construct your store and that your store front will be alongside other retailers in a dedicated shopping environment and retailing community.

Buying a parcel alongside a busy venue seems a great idea until the venue moves or shuts, the land is sold and the sim transformed overnight into a wilderness! We should also consider that succeeding in Second Life is largely about experimentation and adaptability. A particular project may not perform well and it remains important to growth and success to be able to abandon our non-performing ideas for revised concepts.

As always it is important to check the credentials (as far as you can!) of any resident you intend to buy or rent land from (except when buying on the Mainland, as Gov. Linden is considered a very responsible landlord). If a Private Estate owner evicts you, then you will have no option (bar begging) to either challenge the decision or reclaim any fees paid. It will prove equally frustrating if your landlord doesn't or can't pay their own monthly Second Life maintenance charges (tier) as you will also lose your space when Linden Lab reclaim their land.

Be particularly wary of entering agreements with new residents. They may not be dishonest, but they may be suffering under some 'Grand Plan' delusion. When their dream comes tumbling down you do not want your more considered strategy to be caught in the collapse.

Find out how secure your prospective landlord is, for your landlord is your first business partner. Any success you achieve will be compounded by securing a decent and secure landlord. Speak to other retailers as most will be delighted to share their experiences with other entrepreneurial residents.

Irie tip

When renting privately, unless you have 100% confidence in your landlord, do not pay for any longer periods than is required under their terms in order to minimize your losses in the event of the mall closing.

Location, location, location!

Whether you are thinking of renting or buying your first space, the location of your store is critical. You may have the best products in Second Life but if they are not seen by other residents then you are going to struggle to turn a buck. If you are considering buying a space for your first store, don't!

Use the various Second Life Search functions to explore a number of shopping malls with spaces to rent. Start to examine the options by initially considering the traffic figures of the malls. The Traffic figure is the result of a mystical algorithm reflecting a combination of how many residents visit a particular parcel and how long they remain there and is currently the best available analysis of a parcel's popularity.

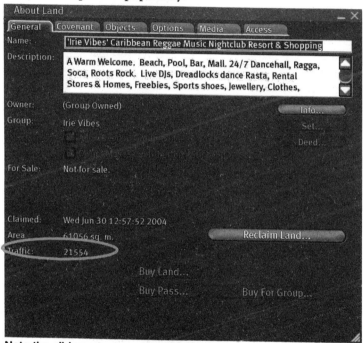

Note the all-important parcel traffic figure

In order to sell products you will need other residents to pass your store front. If you open your first store in a shopping mall with traffic numbers of only a few hundred, you are unlikely to be in a position to attract enough sales to justify the cost.

However, traffic figures can be greatly skewed by camping activities. If the parcel owner is paying residents to remain on a parcel then it becomes safe to assume that the traffic generated will not usually have many spare Linden dollars with which to purchase your products.

Ideally you are looking for a shopping mall that has some synergy with your own ideas and products, has genuine (non-camping) traffic and is operated by a reliable landlord.

A store close to a parcel's main landing point will generate more footfall than if your store takes some finding. For this reason try to ensure that your store is within easy sight of the parcel's Landing Point. If not, assess how and if visitors move around the parcel. If you can find an available store beside a busy walkway or attraction, then this can often be just as suitable as being positioned by the parcel's landing zone.

Open store fronts present better visibility and nice styling pleases the eye. Assess the professionalism of the operation. Is the notecard sane, neat and presentable?

Check how many prims are available with the store, what privileges and permissions store tenants are assigned. Is the store, for example, on its own little land parcel meaning the tenant can play their own music, create there own landing zone, etc.? You will need to decide which abilities are important to your enterprise and evaluate these options accordingly.

Check out your prospective neighbours... Can you grab a store next to an existing 'hot' retailer? That would certainly help your own visibility. Oh, and nightmare neighbours exist in Second Life too! Are any adjacent vendors spewing annoying chat and text into the store that you are considering? That might be an off-putter.

Store design and layout

Navigating Second Life in tight spots can be tricky even for the most experienced residents. Stores with lots of doors, walkways, low ceilings, etc. play havoc with the default camera views so look to have open frontage, high ceilings and open spaces within which residents can comfortably operate and easily browse your products.

Wide doors and high ceilings allow for comfortable browsing

It is your products that you will want to stand out, not the store build and not the vendors. Poor texturing and/or irregular patterns attract the eye. The purpose of good store design is that customer focus remains on the products.

A neat and professional layout speaks volumes for your business. If a store looks like a dump then residents may assume that both the quality of the products and the customer service may also be poor.

Renting the space

Once you have found your perfect spot it is time to rent the space. Most rental stores have automated payment boxes which when clicked manage the transaction and also often deliver a notecard outlining any terms and conditions. Examine these carefully, then open the Covenant tab of the parcel's About Land window to familiarize yourself with any further restrictions. Ensure that your store and products obey the parcels restrictions, terms and conditions. If you break a parcel's terms you run the risk of being evicted without discussion or refund.

Once the store is rented you may also need to join a group in order to place your objects. Details will be on the notecard (if not then IM the owner or manager).

When you are renting a store, you are securing some space and an allocation of the parcel's available prims. The cost of renting a small store currently ranges upwards from about L$5 per prim per week for as few as 20 prims. But let us assume we need 50 prims and they will cost us L$400 per week i.e. L$8 per prim per week. This is a great starting position and not a bad price for a well-located small store. Paying upwards of L$10 per prim per week is not unusual in prime locations and can still prove profitable. Rental rates can reduce to as little as L$2–3 per prim per week when leasing large 1,000 prim stores for example. But that is not for now.

Selling your products in-world

Once we have secured some store-space we need to find a method of selling our Second Life products. We could just place an object we wish to sell in the store then check the **For Sale** box on the **General** tab of its **Edit** window (selecting the Copy radio button so as not to lose the original). But for any object that exceeds one prim (or an item that is not an object, e.g. Second Life clothing, animations, etc.) then this is not a practical solution, for example some hair pieces are well over 100 prims and using this method would mean that each product would need a large store to itself. Additionally, some products, such as a pair of shoes, consist of more than one item and again selling them using this method proves impractical. We may also wish to include a landmark and/or notecard with each purchase and this method does not allow for this option.

Vending boxes

The more practical and common solutions to selling multi-prim or multi-item products are to use vending boxes or purpose-designed vending systems.

The cheapest and simplest (workable) method to sell an item is to box the item(s):

1 Create (render) a prim to serve as the vendor.

2 From the inventory set the product's item permissions (i.e. Copy, Modify, Transfer).

3 Drag the item(s) from your inventory into the **Contents** tab of the prim serving as the vendor.

4 Drag any landmark, notecard, texture, etc. you wish to include with the sale into the **Contents** tab of the vendor prim.

Check that you are satisfied with the permissions of all items listed in the Contents tab.

5 Design and create a texture to apply to the prim serving as the vendor. Textures for vendors should all be 512 × 512 pixels maximum and preferably 256 × 256 pixels or even less. Higher resolution textures take longer to load. There is no point in having your store right by the landing zone if your textures don't load quickly as in all likelihood your potential customers will have moved away. Include on the vendor's texture, a description of the product and the status of the item permissions. I usually do not include the price for if I wish to adjust a price at a later stage then I would then need to create a new texture.

Clean, clear and building brand identity

6 (Optional) Create a simple 'set text' script to display floating text above the prim serving as the vendor.

7 Display the **General** tab of the **Edit** window of the prim serving as the vendor then name the object, tick the **For Sale** checkbox and set a price.

8 Select the **Contents** radio button.

9 Select **Buy Object** from the **When Left-Clicked:** dropdown menu (also on the General tab).

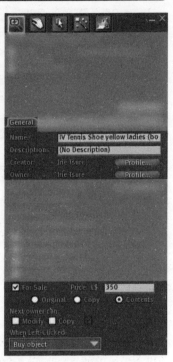

Networked vending systems

Purchasing (or even scripting!) a networked vending system allows us to sell products throughout Second Life. The network consists of a *server*, into which we place products, and *vendors* located across Second Life to display and sell our products. When a customer pays or clicks a vendor for information, the vendor contacts the server to deliver the item or information notecard. This means residents can sell items in as many locations as we wish yet only have to update the inventory of one server.

Networked vendors available for purchase in Second Life offer features such as:

- We can set up and manage products and vendors online by visiting a website to edit prices, descriptions, notecards, etc.

- We can keep all our retail items in-world in a single server.

- With certain packages, we can sell other residents' products and earn a commission.

- With certain packages, we can make our products available for other residents to sell from their vendors.

- With certain packages, we can sell our products online.

- Vendors can cycle automatically through products as a slideshow.

- The system can be set to share sales income with partners.

- The system can categorize and group products into ranges so we can control which appear on individual vendors.

- We can track our sales using online sales logs.

Networked vendors can be expensive, but there are free networked vendor systems which charge commission on sales of your products. I suggest producing box vendors to sell your items until you are in a position to purchase a non-commission version.

As your empire expands you will almost certainly consider a networked vending system because visiting many stores scattered across the grid is much more time-consuming than managing your stock from a central server and from a web page.

Irie note

The urban myth that networked vending systems create unmanageable levels of lag can be a nuisance and some less-learned mall operators do not allow them. The reality is that the bling earrings on the avatar walking through the store are likely to be creating more load than any amount of vendors sited within the store.

Setting prices

You have choices in strategy when it comes to setting your prices. On the one hand you may choose to sell a product cheaply and count on high volume sales, but on the other you may elect to set a more expensive price tag for your products but anticipate selling fewer or to choose to set some other price in between. Research similar products already in the marketplace (if there are any) and set your price as you feel best. Over time, don't be shy about altering and experimenting with your prices to examine how this affects your income. It's called holding a sale!

Perceived value is very important to Second Life residents but if you have a unique or specialist product you may be able to command much higher prices. This inflated effect reduces over time either as alternatives, or heaven forbid, even improvements, to your concept are released by other residents.

Shop assistants

A few store operators employ other residents as shop assistants or sales representatives. Customer service at the point of sale holds many obvious advantages over vending machines and your employees need not be tied to a specific location.

Retailing Second Life products online

It is also worth retailing products and services via the websites of Second Life product aggregators such as SL Exchange, OnRez and Apez. Many residents searching for specific items, choose to do much of their shopping from such websites rather than visiting stores in-world.

Opening a resort or nightclub

Operating a nightclub or music venue is certainly one of the more attractive, commonly attempted but most challenging aspirations a resident can undertake. The reality is that only a handful of Second Life venues have managed to maintain the owner's or other residents' attention for more than a few months.

First let us again quickly draw a distinction between a hobby and a business. If your primary ambition is to open a venue for you and your friends to listen to all your favourite tunes or you intend to lay down camping stations so that you can appear to be popular then you are entertaining an expensive hobby and that is great. But we are discussing business and let us not confuse the two. The primary definition of a business in Second Life has to be that the operation makes a profit.

There are very few music venues that cover their own costs. Why is this? My assessment is that the business model employed by most budding club owners is terribly flawed. The notion that a resident can rent a quarter of a sim, throw down a dance-floor, stream Internet radio, hire a few DJs and the venue will flourish, is evidently folly.

Building a successful venue is a lengthy process. To create an income the venue will need to draw residents repeatedly and those residents will need to bring other residents.

It seems no coincidence that the most successful venues in Second Life have grown around a community. It is therefore the community that should be the focus of growth. Success will follow as the venue becomes the community 'hang-out'. In essence, creating a successful venue is more about building a strong community and less about erecting a fancy dancehall.

But running a club is neither a 24-hour party nor an exclusively community vocation; there are many practicalities that need to be attended to. The venue should provide continuity, i.e. someone is usually there in order to welcome patrons and something interesting is often happening. The club needs to be fresh and pleasing on the eye, the build must be high quality, the club also needs staffing, events need organizing and most important, the business model needs an income. The result of putting these roles together means the time invested by successful Second Life club owners is considerable.

The preparation

So let us consider opening a brand new nightclub. What are we going to need?

1 **A fresh idea** – We cannot produce an inferior and less populated copy of an existing and more successful venue. We will need a new angle.

2 **Building and scripting skills** – Pumping large amounts of Linden dollars into the business is a terrible habit to form and should be avoided like the plague. After a few months it is most likely you will become very bored with sinking your cash into your expensive new hobby. Learn to build and script. It is not difficult and you have time. Building and growing a venue is a perfect arena in which to rapidly increase your knowledge and to develop a wide range of creative and business skills.

3 **Land** – We will need a space that permits us to operate a nightclub.

4 **Entertainment** – We need to provide the necessary motivation for residents to visit and revisit our venue.

5 **Income streams** – This is no hobby! Our venue needs to be funding itself reasonably soon after opening (let's say within a couple of months).

6 **Money** – Though we intend keeping our costs to a minimum, there is going to be an investment required to set up our venue and maintain it during the first couple of months, e.g. rent.

The idea

As with all businesses you will either need an original idea for your venue or have an angle that will improve an experience currently available to residents. Sound difficult? I don't think so. The virtual experience of Second Life is in its infancy, there are currently not many successful clubs and as such almost all the opportunities still lay waiting to be grasped.

Start small

One of the fastest routes to failure is to prejudge the marketplace. You may love your venue idea, your plans may be grand but as previously stated, the marketplace is the only significant judge. Do not be tempted to invest in a huge space. A vast empty club is hardly an atmospheric environment for patrons or inspiring for you as the owner. Do not buy quarter or half of a sim, or even worse secure a whole one in order to test your 'Indie club with Elf-Biker theme' theory. Land in Second Life is not cheap and your income will almost certainly fall spectacularly short of your costs. The key to in-world entrepreneurial success is to cover your costs and in order to do that we need to grow the venue organically from a small but relatively risk-free base. A small intimate, busy, thriving and growing venue is our initial goal and as it happens a 1024 sq. m. parcel of land is a sensible and ample area to initially test the idea.

As with a retail outlet, your best approach is to start by renting a parcel from a reliable landlord, where there are no restrictive covenants on the parcel.

Design and layout

Please... use your imagination... anything but a dark box with a square dance-floor in the middle! And I'm pretty sure it isn't compulsory to have pole-dancers. Take the time to create a stylish and uniquely interesting venue. Please the eye and remember that generally 'less is more'. Never buy a prefabricated club and don't employ a builder. Build it yourself for you have the time. If you don't think you will have the time to learn to build and script then you certainly will not have the time to develop a flourishing venue. Most importantly, this will be *your* venue and therefore should always reflect *your* evolving vision.

Start with a basic shape, try to incorporate some curves or other non-cube shapes into the building to provide uniqueness and interest, then over the following days, weeks, months and ultimately years, tinker, change, adapt and evolve the design. Your skills will develop rapidly and your venue will maintain its freshness. Take the time to create a Second Life highlight!

Streaming music into Second Life

The simplest and free method of broadcasting music across your parcel is to stream a public Internet radio station.

For this example we use **Winamp** (www.winamp.com) or the **Windows Media Player** to tune into an Internet radio station that both broadcasts a relevant musical genre 24 hours a day and is light on advertising. You will find such Internet radio stations either using your preferred search engine or by visiting www.shoutcast.com which has an impressive catalogue of public Internet radio stations.

1 Once the Internet radio station is playing properly on your system (not within Second Life) either:

For **Winamp:**

2 Access the Winamp **MP3 Stream Info Box** with a right-click on the player's top menu bar, then select **View File Info...** from the drop-down menu.

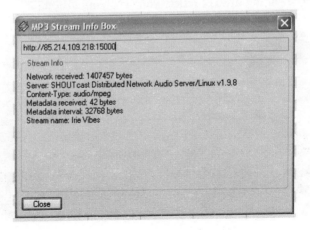

3 Copy the stream URL ([Ctrl] + [C]) that appears in the first field of the displayed **MP3 Stream Info Box**.

Irie tip

I suggest selecting a 96Kbps (or less) radio stream as streaming at a higher bit-rate can cause the music to stutter for residents with limited bandwidth and/or older, slower systems.

For Windows Media Player:

2 Access the Windows Media Player **Properties** with a right-click on the top menu bar then select **File > Properties** from the drop-down menu.

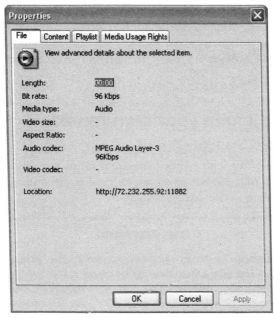

3 Copy the stream URL ([Ctrl] + [C]) that appears in the **Location** field of the displayed Properties dialog box.

4 Paste this stream URL ([Ctrl] + [V]) into the Music URL field in the Media tab of the parcel's 'About Land' window.

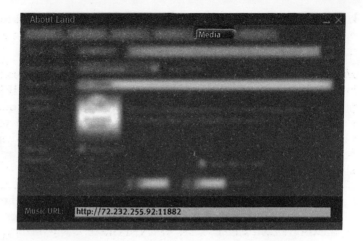

Music URL: http://72.232.255.92:11882

If an invalid URL is entered into the Music URL field there will
be silence but you will not be notified with any error message. If
this happens then enter the stream URL into an external media
player such as Winamp to confirm that the URL is broadcasting
properly.

Streaming in your own music

We stream our own music into Second Life by using a streaming
relay server. We send a single stream of music from our computer system to the relay server which then relays multiple copies
of the stream to our parcel visitors.

Irie warning!

If you choose to stream your own media (music, video, etc.)
into Second Life either directly or using a streaming relay
host then the content and any copyright/royalty fees as well
as any other possible issues are solely your responsibilities.

The most common streaming solutions are Shoutcast, Icecast
and Nicecast for the Mac OS. There are in-world businesses who
rent these relay servers to residents. Due to the amount of bandwidth required for multiple streaming, the price of renting a re-

lay server varies depending on the quality of stream you wish to provide (e.g. 96 Kbps) and your venue requirements (i.e. the maximum number of simultaneous listeners you anticipate).

Many broadcasters use professional DJ software to play the music but this is an expensive option. Alternatively the Winamp MP3 player with a Shoutcast DSP plug-in (both available free from www.winamp.com) can be used to broadcast our MP3s or to perform live music using the line-in socket on our system soundcard. Information on using Winamp to broadcast to a relay server is available from their website.

Irie newsflash!

A new kid has recently arrived on the block to compete for the attention of Second Life's broadcasters. **MediaMaster** (www.mediamaster.com) offers a web-based storage facility to which we can currently upload an unlimited number of music tracks. A web-based control panel is used to sort and arrange these files into playlists. The real advantage is that MediaMaster also provides a 'radio' facility that supplies us with a URL with which to access our stored files and playlists. This can be entered into our Second Life parcel's music URL field, and the result is that as a venue owner I can now broadcast my own music files without my own computer system being involved in the process. Media-Master may not be as versatile a system as streaming from our own computer systems (i.e. is not suitable for DJing), but (for me) acts as a near-perfect solution for providing parcel 'radio' in between live sessions.

Developing the business

Using a Second Life group

You should immediately create a group for your outlet or venue to facilitate communications with your customers and community. The Group Roles feature can be used to create distinctive group tags, e.g. we have 'Irie Vibes VIP' tags for all members and 'Irie Vibes Legends' tags for those members that have supported our community beyond the norm.

Irie tip

Carefully examine and edit Group Roles Allowed Abilities (permissions) especially the accounting options. Ensure you, as the owner, are the only resident that receives group income and pays group bills. Unless you have a really good reason not to, then uncheck **Pay group liabilities and receive group dividends'** from all other roles' Allowed Abilities.

Invite as many of your customers as possible to join the group but remember that it is the height of bad manners to invite members to your group from within another resident's premises.

Use the Second Life Group Notice system to announce new products, sales and to deliver complimentary items to customers. (For more on groups, see Chapter 11.)

Organizing events

With a venue, the primary method of encouraging residents to visit and revisit is to organize regular and entertaining events. DJ sessions, live music, parties, competitions, discussions, workshops, etc. can provide the necessary motivation to encourage residents to hang out at the venue and to invite other residents to join them. To start with and to set the tone and style, it is a good idea to provide much of this entertainment personally.

Creating income

As we are only discussing business ventures (and not hobbies), it becomes essential to provide income streams for the venue. If within a few months of opening the required income is not generated to cover the costs of the venue, the evidence of history shows that the owner will not be stimulated enough to maintain the project and the venue will be abandoned.

Make it easy for residents to reward the experience. Create and script highly visible tip-jars for the venue and position them around the areas that patrons congregate.

Make your own products and locate your own store in the best possible position.

Create store and advertising spaces for rent. Start with three or four and once they are rented add two or three more. Do not be tempted to erect 40 stores to start with as the mall will look pretty bleak. It is better to construct a pleasant park alongside a few stores then build further stores as demand dictates.

Try to design your mall so all store spaces are visible from either the parcel Landing Point or another focal point (e.g. a nightclub dance-floor). (See Chapter 9 for more on mall management.)

Minimizing lag

It can be irritating when a blinged-up resident walks into your venue spewing particles and complaining about lag, especially when you have carefully constructed your sim to keep it to a minimum. The only way to eliminate lag entirely is to close your sim to all other residents and don't build anything! Beyond that it is a lag limitation project particularly when the venue is busy.

Irie tip

Irritating though it is to hear complaints, don't fret. Most lag will be client side. Many complaining residents do not understand that they are really stating that their system, be it their computer or their Internet connection, is just not up to running the Second Life software at an acceptable level and the resultant experience is frustrating them.

But as venue owners we should follow the following guidelines to keep lag to minimum levels:

• Build using low resolution textures (512 × 512 maximum).

• Reuse these textures wherever you can.

• Do not use moving objects such as permanently rotating turntables or permanently 'pumping' speakers).

• Be sparing with your use of rotating lights and objects, animated textures, flashing lights, etc.

• Use efficient scripts (**see scripting**). Avoid permanently open listeners and sensors in particular.

Community

Assuming that we succeed in keeping residents visiting our venue, over time our group will have evolved, friendships formed, stores opened, support offered and help requested. A community has been born. If this community thrives then so will your venue.

Identifying what attributes will benefit a community is a very imprecise science and is highly dependent upon each community's common values, aspirations and interests. But I would suggest that you consider the following ideas to maintain a sense of community within your group and venue.

Have firm rules...

Identify the standards that best reflect the community and stamp on any behaviour that will fundamentally upset the environment for other patrons.

... But not too many

A raft of other more ridiculous rules and regulations for patrons or tenants to observe reeks of a venue owner flaunting their power. No bling! No AO! No this and no that are not inviting welcomes. I've even heard an owner instruct that only English be spoken! I doubt that he is a club owner any longer or if he is then I imagine that he is dancing alone.

Create a welcoming environment

Many residents are actively searching for a community but may be shy. They are far more likely to return to a venue if they feel welcome there. Be there to greet and chat with visitors. If a resident offers you their friendship then accept it. Your friends list has no limits and you can disable the 'Such and such a resident has just logged on/off' message from your Preferences window.

Create a comfortable environment

Set the tone. Instigate and maintain conversations, lead the fun and laughter. Be respectful, tolerant and as involved as possible. You are the venue owner and most residents will understand that you may often be busy but it will be noticed as and when you do have the time and energy to involve yourself. When you see a resident hovering on the periphery of proceedings, take a moment to engage and involve them. Make a friend.

Encourage stake-holding

Allow members and tenants to host their own (appropriate) events within your venue. Ask them for help, ideas and support. Residents who feel a sense of belonging, value and/or involvement with the community will strengthen it and provide features and content that will benefit everyone.

Staff

If you are running a resort, hiring good staff is essential for growth. As a venue develops it becomes impossible to handle all the roles personally. Your staff will act as your personal and the venue's representatives and it is therefore crucial that you consider your prospective staff very carefully.

Irie tip

Hire staff from your regulars. They are already supporting the community by being there and in my experience are often delighted to support the community further.

Second Life wages are almost always derisory but are important as they serve as a token of your personal appreciation and allow some residents to finance their own in-world existence.

Never ever forget that the only reason people will work at a venue is because they want to! You will be unable to pay them more than a pittance so setting tight schedules, exerting authority, over-burdening or under-burdening them (so they stand around doing nothing), allowing them to feel uninvolved, undervalued or upsetting them in any other way will drive good staff away. You might be the boss but they don't need you. You need them.

Communicate regularly with your staff in order to find out whether they are enjoying their role. Would they like to do more? Or less? Do they have any ideas, suggestions or problems they would like to raise? Support your staff and they will support you and the community.

Most staff will drift away eventually so always be on the look-out for enthusiastic and appropriate members who may be interested in supporting the community further by acting as staff members.

Irie tip

Over time I have learned that staff members usually perform better when tasked with short projects rather than overall roles. For example asking a staff member to organize one event next Thursday will normally get you a great event next Thursday. Asking someone to organize an event every Wednesday will often result in a few good Wednesdays then a tail-off in attention as other commitments and opportunities surpass your requirements. Of course if a staff member shows great commitment to their individual events then it is certainly worth asking them if they would like to schedule something more regular.

Staff responsibilities may include:

• Inviting residents to join the Second Life group.

• Greeting residents as they arrive.

• Maintaining the conversation and atmosphere in the venue.

• Hosting events.

• Managing conflict and ejecting troublemakers.

• Managing the venue's entertainment.

Onwards and upwards

Once your business, income stream and community are established it becomes time to consider more space. Work within your Second Life income stream to expand, i.e. when your income from one unit provides the money to comfortably invest in another then do so and not before. With success you will be able to finance additional outlets, or venues for your community's use and eventually perhaps move to your own sim (or two).

As the venue grows and your reputation develops you should consider a larger mall and other land management ventures.

09 land management

In this chapter you will learn:

- how to buy and manage land
- how to make money from virtual land
- how to minimize lag on your land

About virtual land

Second Life residents acquire virtual land parcels on which they erect their homes and run their businesses. Second Life land is defined as either **Mainland** or **Private Estate** (aka Private Islands) and rated as either **PG** or **Mature**.

The PG and Mature ratings of regions reflect the standards used in the movie industry to denote the age-appropriateness of a given region of Second Life and do not imply that children (U18) are welcome in certain regions of Second Life (older kids can use the Teen Second Life grid). The PG regions intend to offer adult residents an experience free of content such as sexually explicit or violent language, behaviour and imagery.

The **Mainland** is made up of the continents in the middle of the World Map. Mainland is designed, rated and leased to residents by Linden Lab and all Mainland tier payments (monthly maintenance and usage fees) are paid directly to Linden Lab.

Irie note

To own Mainland, a resident must register for a Premium Second Life account using the **Upgrade/Downgrade Account** page accessible from the **My Account** page of the Second Life website.

Residents may own as much Mainland as they choose and then use this land without restrictions other than the region rating and Second Life's TOS. When we change the amount of Mainland we own then the monthly tier payment to Linden Lab will adjust accordingly. A resident's tier payment reflects their peak land ownership during the previous month and is charged by Linden Lab automatically each month. Residents can view their current land holdings, tier and account information from the My Account page of the Second Life website.

Finding land for sale

Residents have several choices when it comes to identifying land for sale.

From Search

The **Land Sales** tab of the **Search** window ([Ctrl] + [F]) displays a list of all the land parcels that residents have up for sale.

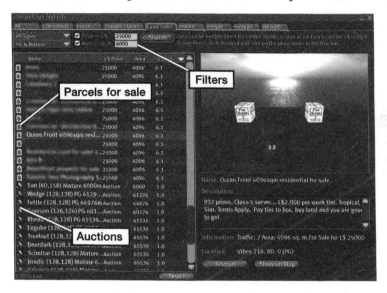

The **All Types** and **PG & Mature** drop-down menus can be used to filter these results by the type of land sale (i.e. Mainland, Estate or Auction) and by the region rating. The results can be filtered further by parcel area and price by entering a maximum spend and/or a minimum area into the relevant filter field.

From the World Map

When we tick the **Land for Sale** checkbox on the World Map legend, areas on the World Map ([Ctrl] + [M]) that are overlain in yellow identify land parcels for sale. Areas on the World Map that are overlain in purple indicate land parcels for Second Life auction (see below).

The small $ price-tag icon often seen within an overlain area can be clicked on in order to display some basic details of the sale.

It is imperative to carefully examine any land parcel you are interested in purchasing in order to ascertain if it is well suited

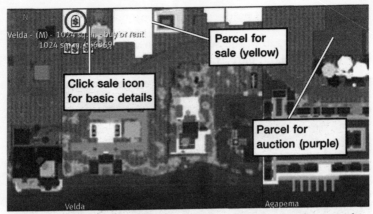

to your own purposes. Make the following checks (from within the parcel) prior to confirming any land purchase:

- Select **World** > **About Land** from the viewer's top menu bar and confirm the parcel's **Area** figure from the **General** tab. This value describes the size of the parcel in square metres.

- From the **Objects** tab of the About Land window examine the **Primitives Parcel Supports** figure. This is one of the most important values to consider as it indicates how many prims may be placed on this parcel (the parcel's prim limit).

- To ensure that we are aware of the exact size and shape of the parcel, we can display the parcel boundaries from either the viewer's top toolbar **View** > **Property Lines** or by using the keyboard shortcut **[Ctrl]** + **[Alt]** + **[Shift]** + **[P]**.

- If large or numerous objects are obscuring your view of the parcel then we can hide pretty much everything except the land itself by displaying the viewer's **Advanced** menu (**[Ctrl]** + **[Alt]** + **[D]**) then un-selecting **Advanced** > **Rendering** > **Types** > **Volume** (**[Ctrl]** + **[Alt]** + **[Shift]** + **[9]**).

Buying land in Second Life

When we are on a parcel that is for sale we can purchase it by clicking the **Buy** icon on the viewer's top menu bar or **Buy Land...** on the **General** tab of the parcel's **About Land** window.

The **Buy Land** window opens, displaying the full details of the transaction and also informing the purchaser whether completing the transaction will require them to upgrade their Second Life account and/or commit them to an increased monthly tier.

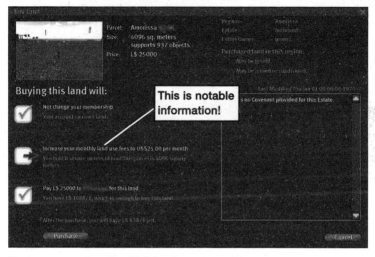

Buying a parcel on the Mainland

The transaction is completed by clicking the **Purchase** button.

Buying land from private estates

When considering buying land within a private estate it is crucial to be aware that there are fundamental differences between buying Mainland parcels and private estate parcels.

Parcels within private estates are governed by estate covenants. These may outline conditions such as themes, payment terms, rules, regulations and permitted behaviours within the estate boundaries. Before being permitted to buy the land parcel, the purchaser may need to agree to them by ticking the **I Agree to the Covenant Defined Above** checkbox. Always ensure that you read, understand and accept the estate covenant before you buy any parcel. If you do not adhere to any regulation contained within a private estate covenant then you run the real risk of being evicted from your parcel without discussion or refund.

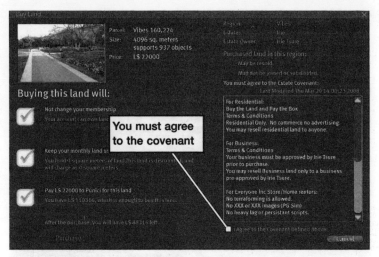

Buying a parcel on a private estate

One of the potential benefits to buying land in a private region is that land management fees (tier charges) are charged independently from Second Life, i.e. buying land in a private region does not affect a resident's Second Life account land tier rating. Therefore a resident need not necessarily subscribe to a Premium Second Life account in order to own a land parcel within a Private Estate. However the Private Estate owner is almost certain to levy their own tier charge.

One of the potential downsides to buying land in a Private Region is that the Estate owner can evict a resident and reclaim the parcel at any time.

Irie warning!

Do not buy land parcels within private regions if you are not totally confident in the reliability of the estate owner. We too regularly hear the sorry tales of leaseholders being evicted with no notice even when long periods of tier have been paid in advance. Linden Lab will not involve themselves in any such dispute and the evicted resident has no open avenue of redress. Also if an estate owner does not maintain their own tier payments to Linden Lab you will lose your parcel when the region is reclaimed.

Buying land by auction

New Mainland regions and repossessed parcels are released to residents by Linden Lab through an auction system accessed via the Second Life website. Residents may enter a maximum bid for a parcel then the automatic auctioning system will bid in turn for each resident until their maximum bid is reached. At the end of the auction the successful bidder's account will be charged and the land parcel assigned to them.

Selling land in Second Life

Residents can set for sale any land parcel they own (or that their group owns if they have been granted the ability to sell group land) with a click on the **Sell Land...** button on the **General** tab of the parcel's **About Land** window. **The Sell Land** window opens into which we enter the details of the sale.

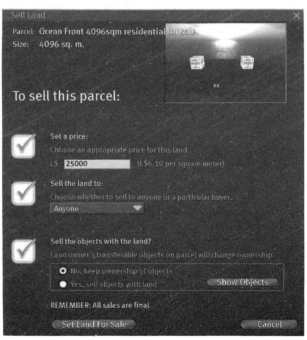

In the **Set a price:** field we enter the price (in Linden dollars) at which we want to sell the parcel. The cost per square metre is automatically calculated and displayed alongside this field.

We specify whether we want to sell the land to anyone or to a particular Resident from the **Sell the land to:** drop-down menu.

Irie warning!

If you ever intend to sell a land parcel to a specific Second Life resident (especially if at a knock-down price) then always ensure that you select 'Specific user:' from the **Sell the land to:** drop-down menu. Some cunning residents operate perfectly legitimate software that detects bargain land parcels the moment they become publicly available.

By selecting one of the radio buttons in the **Sell the objects with the land?** section of the **Sell Land** window, the seller also has the option to transfer to the purchaser any objects that they own on the parcel (subject to each object's permissions). This is particularly useful when selling a parcel that includes a building and/or landscaping. We can highlight any objects that will change ownership by clicking the **Show Objects** button.

Click on the **Set Land For Sale** button to confirm the details and set the parcel for sale. Unless the land is set for sale to a specific resident the parcel will automatically be displayed in the listings of the **Land Sales** tab of the Search window ([Ctrl] + [F]).

Obtaining a private island

Though I implore you not to buy a vast space until your Second Life income provides for it, we do intend that your entrepreneurial endeavours will in time lead you to require more and more space. As the time comes for you to consider a whole region then you must decide whether your new sim will be bought by auction on the Mainland or whether now is the time to have your very own sim created.

A Second Life **Private Estate** is managed and operated separately from the mainland. Estate owners purchase from Linden Lab entire regions (commonly referred to as *private islands*) away from the Mainland either for their own use, or to divide then sell or rent sub-divisions to other residents.

Estate owners are able to control many more aspects of their land than can mainland landowners. Private estate owners may for example, adjust or halt the sun cycle, change the region rating or regulate the total number of avatars permitted on the sim (40 max. on a Mainland region against 100 max. on a private island). Estate owners can also add a Covenant to a region designating their own specific estate rules and conditions (see page 138).

Second Life residents buy entire private regions using the Land Store which is accessed via the Second Life website. When we purchase a region from the Second Life Land Store we get to name the region and rate it as either PG or M (mature). Without our permission, other residents cannot buy adjacent regions to our new region which leaves us free to add to the estate as our community and requirements dictate.

Owning a private region is more expensive than maintaining an equivalent space on the Second Life Mainland but brings with it a whole raft of enviable 'god-like' powers not available to owners of Mainland regions. These include the abilities to:

- Fix the position of the sun
- Adjust the sun-cycle
- Increase the region's capacity to 100 avatars
- Change the region's rating
- Set an Estate covenant
- Restart the region
- Edit ground textures
- Change the water height
- Send pop-up messages to our visitors
- Reclaim land on the estate (see below)
- Own 'Openspaces'.

Openspaces (void regions)

Whereas normal regions run on their own dedicated CPU, the Openspace regions run four per CPU and are limited to only 3,750 prims each (a Second Life Region usually supports 15,000 prims). Openspace regions are suitable for those estate owners wishing to offer 'light use' areas such as open water for boating, sailing, etc. Linden Lab do not support more intense use than this and will not respond to reports of performance issues should the owner use an Openspace for more concentrated activities such as events or stores.

Managing private regions

Once we own one or more private regions we control many of the estate features from the **Region/Estate** window accessed by standing in our region then selecting **World > Region/Estate** from the viewer's top menu bar.

The **Estate** tab of the Region/Estate window manages options that affect an entire estate which may comprise one or more regions. The remaining tabs manage options specific to the region we are currently in.

The Region tab

- **Block Terraform:** Ticking this checkbox prevents any resident other than the estate owner from terraforming anywhere in the region irrespective of any contained parcel's **Edit Terrain** setting (**About Land > Options** tab).

- **Block Fly:** Ticking this checkbox prevents any resident other than the Estate owner from flying within the region irrespective of any contained parcel's **Allow other residents to: Fly** setting (**About Land > Options** tab).

- **Allow Damage:** Ticking this checkbox allows residents to suffer 'damage' throughout the region irrespective of any contained parcel's **Land Options: Safe (no damage)** setting (**About Land > Options** tab). Avatar damage is a Second Life feature most commonly used when residents are engaging in multi-player combat games within combat-defined regions.

- **Restrict Pushing:** Collisions are one of the physics features of the Second Life grid. To avoid disruptive or aggressive behaviour within a region the owner can prevent pushing (caused by collisions) by ticking this checkbox. This applies throughout the region irrespective of any contained parcel's **Land Options: Restrict Pushing** setting (**About Land > Options** tab).

- **Allow Land Resell:** Ticking this checkbox allows residents who purchase land within the region to sell it on to other residents or deed it to groups.

- **Allow Parcel Join/Divide:** Ticking this checkbox allows residents who purchase land within the region to subdivide and join their parcels.

- **Agent Limit:** This field specifies the maximum number of avatars that can be contained within the region at any given moment. Estate owners can raise this value to 100. Be aware that large numbers of avatars is likely to increase server load and therefore increase server-side lag.

- **Object Bonus:** The maximum number of prims that a region can support is 15,000. This limit cannot be increased. There are times however when it is useful to increase an individual parcel's prim limit. If the Object Bonus value is set to 1.000 (default) then a 512 sq. m/ parcel supports 117 prims. If the value is increased to 2.000 then a 512 sq. m/ parcel will support 234 prims (though the overall prim limit for the Region remains unchanged at 15,000). I use this feature to permit residents who lease space for large main-stores to cram large quantities of prims into a smaller parcel and this allows me to keep large open beach areas for communal use whilst not wasting the prim allocation.

- **Maturity:** Select from this drop-down menu to establish whether the Region is PG rated or Mature.

- **Teleport Home One User:** Clicking this button allows us to return an undesirable resident back to their home location (right-clicking the avatar then selecting **More > Eject** I find both quicker and more effective as I can also ban the resident from that menu system).

Irie tip

Unless you actually want an argument, Mute any resident you eject, ban or teleport home prior to kicking them out.

- **Teleport Home All Users:** Clicking this button allows us to send all residents in the Region back to their home locations. This feature is used for maintenance and, my guess is, for severe bad moods.

- **Send Message to Region:** Clicking this allows us to send a pop-up message to all residents in the region. I love this and use it regularly to relay personal messages to our guests.

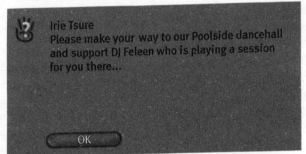

Irie Tsure
Please make your way to our Poolside dancehall and support DJ Feleen who is playing a session for you there...

OK

- **Manage Telehub:** Clicking this button allows us to set a telehub in order to compel all visitors to appear at a defined location. Telehubs are referenced to an object and therefore repositioning the telehub object moves the region's arrival point. Spawn points are other locations set within the region that relate to the main telehub object and therefore move relative to any repositioning of the region's telehub.

To use a telehub we must first un-tick **Allow Direct Teleport** from the **Estate** tab of the **Region/Estate** window and clear any Landing Points set for all the region's parcels.

Irie tip

Under most circumstances using the individual parcel's landing point (About Land > Options tab > Teleport Routing) drop-down menu seems a simpler and more versatile way to direct arriving traffic.

The Debug tab

* **Disable Scripts:** Ticking this checkbox halts all running scripts in the Region.

* **Disable Collisions:** Ticking this checkbox stops the physics engine from calculating object collisions within the region.

* **Disable Physics:** Ticking this checkbox switches off the region's physics engine but has the effect of stopping avatars from moving.

* Clicking the **Choose Avatar** button opens the **Choose Resident** window. On the Debug tab, two wide buttons become active once an individual resident has been selected from this window. Using these buttons, we can return either all of the selected residents' scripted objects or just those scripted objects not contained within parcels they own.

* Clicking the **Get Top Colliders** and **Get Top Scripts** buttons opens a window that lists the physics-enabled and scripted objects with a measure of the load they place upon the region's server. Region owners can use this feature to identify and locate any problem objects that are creating undue load on the server and if necessary return them.

* Clicking the **Restart Region** reboots the region's server. Residents remaining in the region after two minutes will be disconnected from the Second Life grid.

* Clicking the **Cancel Restart** button (within two minutes) aborts the Restart Region request.

The Ground Textures tab

The Ground Textures tab is used to edit the appearance of the region's ground at different elevations and within its different areas. Regions have four levels of ground texture that can be applied independently to each of the four region quarters (e.g. the south-west quarter). The **Texture Elevation Ranges** settings are used to define at what height each texture will be applied. We can texture the Region's ground using any 512 × 512 pixels .tga file contained in our Inventory.

Terrain tab

- **Water Height:** This field specifies the height at which water will be displayed.

- **Terrain Raise Limits:** This specifies how many metres above the region's default terrain level residents may terraform to.

- **Terrain Lower Limits:** This specifies how many metres below the default terrain level residents may terraform to.

- Clicking the **Bake Terrain** button establishes the region's current topography as its default or 'baked' topography.

- **Use Estate Sun:** Ticking this checkbox establishes that the region uses the Estate settings for its day/night cycle (see the Estate tab below).

- **Fixed Sun:** Ticking this checkbox fixes the position of the sun. The sun's position in the sky is set moving the **Phase** slider control then clicking the **Apply** button.

The Estate tab

As mentioned, the Estate tab offers settings that will affect all regions contained within the estate.

- **Estate:** The name of the estate containing this region is displayed in this field (not to be confused with the Region Name).

- **Owner:** The name of the owner of the estate containing this region is displayed in this field.

- **Use Global Time:** Ticking this checkbox establishes that the estate uses the global Second Life day/night cycle.

- **Fixed Sun:** Ticking this checkbox fixes the position of the sun for the Estate. The sun's position in the sky is set moving the **Phase** slider control then clicking the Apply button.

- **Public Access:** Ticking this checkbox permits all Second Life residents to access the estate. By ticking the relevant checkbox from the **Restrict Access To:** subsection, the estate owner can then restrict access based on whether Linden Lab has a resident's payment information on file and/or whether the resident is an age-verified adult.

- **Allow Voice Chat**: Ticking this checkbox permits all voice-enabled residents to use the Voice feature within the Estate.

- **Allow Direct Teleport**: Ticking this checkbox allows other residents to teleport directly to a location selected from the World Map.

- **Abuse email address**: Entering a valid email address in this field will result in abuse reports for the estate being delivered to that email address rather than to Linden Lab's support.

- **Send Message to Estate**: Clicking this button allows the owner to send a pop-up message to all residents in the estate.

- **Kick User from Estate**: Clicking this button allows the estate owner to return an undesirable resident back to their home location.

- **Estate Managers**: Any resident that the estate owner assigns to the role of Estate Manager will be able to control almost all the **Region/Estate** window settings and features and is also considered by Linden Lab to be authorized to request certain region functions such as rollbacks (restoring its appearance and prim content to a previous point in time). Estate managers can also set parcels for sale and change the covenant. I suggest you think long and hard before assigning this role and allowing another resident into the estate's 'circle of trust'.

- **Allowed Residents**: When the **Allow Public Access**: checkbox is not ticked, the Estate owner may add specific residents to the **Allowed Residents** list by clicking the **Add...** button then selecting a resident from the **Choose Resident** window.

- **Allowed Groups**: When the **Allow Public Access**: checkbox is not ticked, the Estate owner may add specific groups to the **Allowed Groups** list by clicking the **Add...** button then selecting a group from the **Groups** window.

- **Banned Residents**: The owner may ban specific residents from the estate by adding them to the **Banned Residents** list by clicking the **Add...** button then selecting the resident by name from the displayed **Choose Resident** window. The estate owner can also eject and ban residents by right-clicking directly on the offender's avatar then selecting **More > Eject...** from their pie menu.

The parcel owner may remove residents from both the **Allowed** and **Banned Resident** lists by selecting their name then clicking the **Remove** button.

The Covenant tab

Sales of land parcels within private estates are usually governed by estate covenants. These may outline conditions such as themes, payment terms, rules, regulations and permitted behaviours within the estate boundaries. It isn't compulsory to set a covenant to enable land sales, but it's wise to set some regulations.

We set or change the covenant by dragging a notecard onto the **Covenant** panel in the **Covenant** tab of the **Region Estate** window. A pop-up will ask you if you are certain. If you are then go ahead and confirm this and the covenant will be reset.

The Edit Terrain menu

Editing topography is commonly referred to as *terraforming*. A parcel can normally only be terraformed by its owner. The owner can also divide a parcel and if a resident owns two or more adjacent parcels then the owner is able to join the parcels together. Editing land in any of these ways is managed using the Edit Terrain tool.

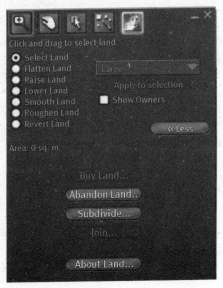

To access the Edit Terrain menu, right-click on the ground of your parcel then select **Edit Terrain** from its pie menu.

If large or numerous objects are obscuring the parcel, you can hide everything except the land by displaying the viewer's

Advanced menu ([Ctrl] + [Alt] + [D]) then un-selecting **Advanced > Rendering > Types > Volume** ([Ctrl] + [Alt] + [Shift] + [9]).

Parcel owners can flatten, raise, lower, smooth or roughen their land. These terraforming effects can be applied to land using one of the following three methods.

To terraform the entire parcel:

1 Select the desired effect radio button, e.g. **Raise Land**.

2 Click the **Apply to selection** button.

In this case, the entire parcel will be raised by approximately a metre.

To terraform a rectangular area within the parcel:

1 Select the **Select Land** radio button.

2 Click on the land, hold down the left button then drag out a rectangle.

3 Release the button when you are happy with the size of the selection.

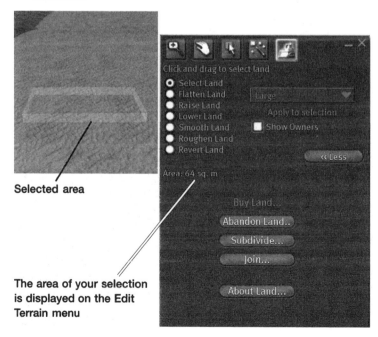

Selected area

The area of your selection is displayed on the Edit Terrain menu

4 Select the desired effect radio button, e.g. **Raise Land**.

5 Click the **Apply to selection** button.

In this example, the land within the selection will be raised by approximately a metre.

To terraform freehand:

1 Select **Small, Medium** or **Large** from the terraforming drop-down menu to choose the size of the area on which you want to apply the terraforming effect.

2 Select the desired effect radio button, e.g. **Raise Land**.

3 Left-click on the land to apply the effect directly.

4 Hold down the left button to apply the effect continuously.

The **Revert Land** option returns a parcel's or a selection's topography to its original 'baked' (recorded) state.

Irie warning!

Be ultra-careful and check you have selected the intended area of land **before** applying any terraforming effect!

Though owners can easily return the topography of a parcel to its original shape, there is no practical method of undoing a single editing step. I have accidently flattened an entire region on a couple of occasions (laying waste to months of tinkering) and this type of terraforming error is both heartbreaking to encounter and time-consuming to remedy.

Ticking the **Show Owners** checkbox applies the following useful colour code to land:

• Bright green land is owned by you.

• Red land is owned by other residents.

• Blue-green land is owned by a group of which you are a member.

• Orange land is for sale.

• Purple land is for sale by auction.

Dividing a parcel

The parcel owner may wish to divide a parcel, for example to sell or rent to other residents.

To divide a parcel:

1 Select the **Select Land** radio button.

2 Click on the land, hold down the left button then drag out a rectangle.

3 Release the button when you are happy with the size of the selection.

4 Click the **Subdivide** button.

The smallest parcel residents may create is 16 sq. m.

Joining parcels

When a resident wants to join together two or more adjacent parcels that they own they simply select the **Select Land** radio button, drag a rectangle to overlap the parcels they wish to join then click the **Join** button.

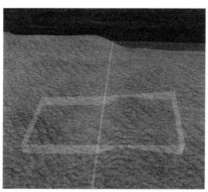

Joining two parcels

The **Abandon Land:** button relinquishes a resident's ownership to the parcel. I suggest that you never abandon land that you can no longer maintain but instead consider giving it to another resident or deeding it to a group.

Making money from virtual land

There are several strategies to making money from Second Life land. The first and most attractive for many residents is to become a 'Land Baron'! Second Life's Land Barons are best known for investing in large parcels of Mainland, buying Mainland regions from auctions or private estates then dividing the land into smaller more manageable spaces which they then either sell or rent to other residents.

The real estate business

Setting up and starting a new Second Life real estate business is costly and not for the faint-hearted. Losses can be enormous compared to other prospective in-world business opportunities and unless a resident knows precisely what they are doing, I can easily envisage losses by the impetuous reaching hundreds and possibly thousands of real-world US dollars.

Each region will cost the estate owner over L$80,000 per month in tier charges alone. That is a lot of income to generate month after month from just one sim. If your business model is to sell parcels of a private estate, then you are going to need to move land quickly in a highly competitive market to cover your monthly costs. The reality is that a resident with no track history may struggle to attract buyers however competitive the rates.

Rather than selling empty parcels, creating a unique, high quality or themed environment may provide an entry point into the market, but in my assessment the best way to profit from this sector is when we sell parcels alongside our existing resident attraction. Such residents already have an established track record, a reputation, a community and potential customers.

Speculating on land prices, i.e. buying land in the hope that we can sell it quickly for a profit, is a gamble. There was a time when every resident (it seemed) was cashing in on spiralling land prices but those days are long gone. Prices do fluctuate but I do not see how they can rise exponentially when demand is hardly likely to outstrip supply when any amount of land can be manifested in an instant with the unlimited creation of new regions.

Managing tenants

Second Life tenants pay a landowner rent for the use of a defined quantity of the parcel's resources. Estate owners may rent defined parcels or a defined number of prims within a parcel.

Estate owners collect rent from tenants using direct payments methods such as PayPal or by using automated rental systems. Automated rental systems available for purchase in Second Life offer features such as:

* We can manage our spaces and rent online.

* We can monitor tenants' prim counts.

* We can automatically remind tenants when their tenancy nears its end.

* We can share income with partners.

* We can categorize and group spaces into groups so we can control and manage parcels by, for example, size or location.

* With certain packages we can track our sales and tenants using online logs.

Settle on the collection method you are most comfortable with then clearly display your payment terms to prospective tenants.

Again if your business model is to rent parcels you are going to need to maintain a healthy occupancy rate in a highly competitive market in order to cover your monthly costs. The reality is that a resident with no track history may struggle to attract tenants however competitive the rates.

Again creating a unique or themed environment may provide an entry point into the rental market but in my assessment the best way to profit from this sector is when we rent parcels alongside our existing resident attraction.

I really don't see selling or renting land as start-up ventures for new residents but more as bolt-on businesses to existing enterprises or communities. If you run an existing venture it may be profitable to consider securing further land in order to sell or rent out parcels.

Managing a shopping mall

Start small

As usual, one of the fastest routes to failure is to prejudge the marketplace. Your plans may be grand but the marketplace is the ultimate and only judge. Do not be tempted to open a huge space. Do not build 50 stores at once, as a vast empty mall is hardly a bustling environment for shoppers or inspiring for you as the owner. Do not buy half a sim or even worse a whole one to test your business model. Land in Second Life is not cheap and your income will almost certainly fall horribly short of your costs. The key to in-world success is to cover your costs and in order to do that we will need to grow organically from a small but relatively risk-free base. Erect maybe half a dozen stores to start with and as those fill then add more. A busy, thriving and growing mall is what we want to achieve in the first instance.

Design your mall so that most if not all stores are either visible from the parcel's landing point or close to the parcel's focal points. Stores with lots of doors, narrow walkways, low ceilings, etc. can play havoc with the default camera views. Look to have open frontage, high ceilings and open spaces in which residents may comfortably and easily browse and operate. Build stores modularly so they are simple to adapt, add to and alter.

Mall operators usually collect rent from their tenants using the automated rental systems described above. A group can be used to give permissions to store tenants to place products without worrying about the parcel's auto-return feature. We can achieve this either by creating a dedicated group for store tenants or by creating a specific role within an existing Second Life group. Either way will need to either set or deed the land parcel to the relevant group.

Write a covenant or notecard which explains the rules and acts as a terms and conditions for your mall. Your conditions should include information such as banned objects (e.g. lag-inducing textures, scripts and products), when payments are due, how flexible you are on late payments, your contact details, etc.

Setting the rent

Do some research into what other mall operators are charging and the necessary maths to ensure that you can cover your costs with (I suggest) 50–60% occupancy. When a tenant rents a store, they are securing both some space and an allocation of your parcel's available prims. Rents for a small store currently costs upwards from about L$5 per prim per week for as few as 20 prims. Rental rates can reduce to as little as L$2–3 per prim per week when leasing larger 1,000 prim stores, for example.

Considering, enquiring and identifying what you can do as a mall operator to benefit storeowners is an important task that should be conducted regularly. If store operators can regularly make a profit in your shopping mall then so should you.

Communicate regularly with your tenants in order to find out whether they have any ideas, suggestions or problems they would like to raise. Support your tenants and they will support you.

Irie tip

DO NOT ask tenants if business is good or whether they are making a profit. This is a dangerous box to open as many retailers will take the opportunity to blame you for poor sales rather than improve their products.

I have managed our mall using the following strategies and although disagreements with store managers have occurred, dispute is extremely rare, as I believe most of our store tenants find me reasonably approachable and also feel secure, valued and comfortable within our retail community.

Be a pleasure to do business with

As a business operator you will be expected to possess a certain professionalism. Be as reliable, reasonable and accommodating (without compromising your own aspirations) as possible. To succeed as a mall operator you need the support of a retailing community. If you are a trustworthy and considerate landlord then the good word may well spread. If you are not responsible then the word is likely to spread faster.

Have firm rules...

Identify the regulations that allow the mall to operate smoothly and stamp on any behaviour that will fundamentally upset the environment for other tenants.

... but not too many

A raft of other more ridiculous rules and regulations for tenants to observe reeks of an owner flaunting their power.

Encourage stake-holding

Allow tenants to host their own (appropriate) events within your shopping mall. Ask tenants for help, ideas and support. Tenants who feel a sense of belonging, value and/or involvement with the community will strengthen the community, provide features and content that will benefit everyone and are more likely to remain as tenants.

Checking region performance

There will be times when it is useful to know how well a region's server is performing. To do this we examine the region's **Frames Per Second** value (Sim FPS) from the **Statistics** bar.

1 Access the **Statistics** menu that relates to the region you are in by selecting **View > Statistics Bar** from the viewer's top menu bar or with the keyboard shortcut [**Ctrl**] + [**Shift**] + [**1**].

2 Ensure that the **Basic** and **Advanced** divisions of the Statistics bar are minimized by left-clicking their title then expand the **Simulator** division again by left-clicking on the title.

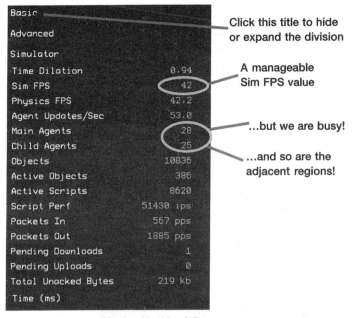

Click this title to hide or expand the division

A manageable Sim FPS value

...but we are busy!

...and so are the adjacent regions!

The Statistics bar ([Ctrl] + [Shift] + [1])

Interpreting Sim FPS values:

* 45 FPS: Perfect!

* 35–44 FPS: This value is fine.

* 20–35 FPS: Our region is performing slowly and the effects are likely to be noticeable.

* 10–20 FPS: Our region is grinding to a halt and resident experience will certainly be very laggy.

* 0–10 FPS: Time to go somewhere else!

The Second Life Statistics bar also presents detailed information about the performance of your computer system and the Second Life grid. The following are some useful statistics in the Simulator division of the Statistics bar (refer to the image above):

* The **Main Agents** line displays **28**. This value reflects the number of avatars currently in the Region. When this value is high it becomes the prime cause of a Region's slow FPS.

- The **Child Agents** line displays 25. This reflects the number of avatars outside your region that can see into it, which can also slow down your region if it's a significant value.

- The **Objects** value indicates the total number of prims in the region. It does not include prims being worn by avatars.

- The **Active Objects** value indicates the number of objects containing active scripts in the region. This value does not include scripts inside attachments being worn by avatars.

- The **Active Scripts** value indicates the number of scripts that are currently running in the region. This value includes scripts inside attachments being worn by avatars.

To further identify any issues that may be slowing down a region, we expand the **Time** sub-division of the Statistics Bar by clicking on the **Time (ms)** title. The following additional region statistics will be displayed:

Time (ms)	
Total Frame Time	22.4ms
Net Time	1.4ms
Sim Time (Physics)	1.1ms
Sim Time (Other)	7.4ms
Agent Time	2.9ms
Images Time	0.3ms
Script Time	8.8ms

The **Total Frame Time** value indicates how long per frame the region's server takes to process all the information that the region is producing.

Interpreting Total Frame Time values:

- Under 22 ms – The region is performing perfectly.

- Very close to 22 ms – The region is performing fine but script processing speed is being sacrificed in order to maintain the overall region frame-rate.

- Over 22 ms – The region is not performing well and even slowing down the rate that scripts are executed is not helping to maintain the overall region frame-rate.

The **Total Frame Time** value is the total of the following 'Time' values:

- **Net Time** – The time per frame spent responding to incoming network data.

- **Sim Time (Physics)** – The time per frame spent running physics, e.g. collisions in the region.

- **Sim Time (Other)** – The time per frame spent managing other region information such as resident movement, environment effects, etc.

- **Agent Time** – The time per frame spent updating object information to avatars.

- **Images Time** – The time per frame spent downloading textures to avatars.

- **Script Time** – The time per frame spent executing scripts.

Improving a region's performance

If you are encountering performance issues with a region then there are several steps that we can take to improve matters.

Textures

In the Statistics bar, the **Images Time** value indicates the time per frame the region's server spends updating texture information to avatars. When residents enter or look into the region they each need to download all the displayed textures from the region server to their Second Life viewer. When a number of avatars are concurrently downloading images, this creates load on the region server and as a result the frame-rate is reduced. If the **Images Time** value is regularly over 2 milliseconds then it becomes worthwhile to perform a little maintenance by:

- Reducing the number of unique textures within the region (use the same textures as often as you can).

- Reducing the resolution of the remaining textures to a maximum of 512 × 512 pixels.

- Reducing the number of animated textures within the region.

Objects

The **Agent Time** value indicates the time per frame the region's server spends updating object data to avatars. Large numbers of objects can slow down a region's performance. Be particularly mindful not to overuse the following load-causing object types:

- Moving objects
- Rotating objects
- Flashing objects
- Morphing objects
- Sculpted prims, twisted tori and other geometrically complex prims
- 'Huge' non-default prims.

Scripts

The **Script Time** value indicates the time per frame the region's server spends running scripts. Inefficient or persistent scripts can hamper a region's performance. If the Script Time value is regularly over 5 milliseconds, it becomes worthwhile to consider:

- Reducing the number of scripts in the region
- Not overusing particle effects
- Not overusing persistent listeners (often found in pose-balls, etc.)
- Not overusing persistent avatar radars and scanners.

Private Estate owners can further examine script activity in a region from the **Debug** tab of the Region/Estate window (**World > Region/Estate**). Clicking the **Get Top Scripts...** button displays the Top Scripts window.

Selecting an object from this list then clicking the **Show Beacon** button will activate an in-world destination beacon indicating the location of the scripted object. Once we have identified any objects that are affecting the region's performance we can then remove, replace or optimize the offending scripts.

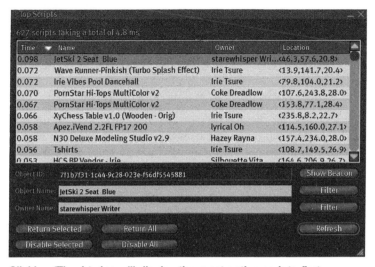

Clicking 'Time' twice will display the most active scripts first

Physics

The **Sim Time (Physics)** value indicates the time per frame the region's server spends calculating collisions. If the **Sim Time (Physics)** value is over 4 milliseconds then it may be worth checking to see if this can be reduced.

Private estate owners can further examine physics activity in a region from the **Debug** tab of the **Region/Estate** window. Clicking the **Get Top Colliders...** button displays the **Top Colliders** window which is very similar in nature to the Top Scripts window we have just discussed.

Again by clicking **Time** twice we display the most active colliders first. Selecting an object from this list then clicking the **Show Beacon** button will activate an in-world destination beacon indicating the location of the collider. Once we have identified any objects that are affecting the region's performance we can then remove them.

Avatars

The **Agent Time** value indicates the time per frame the region's server spends updating object information to avatars. A large number of avatars in a region is likely to be the single biggest factor when it comes to low region frame-rate and this is why regions on the Mainland are limited to holding 40 avatars at any one time. From the **Region** tab of the Region/Estate window, Estate owners can raise this limit as far as 100 avatars or reduce the value in order to maintain region performance.

Though limiting the number of avatars permitted within our region does sound a sensible strategy (because it is) the reality is that as estate-owning venue operators we habitually raise this limit to 100 avatars in the hope that one day we will pack our venue out. Our venue sim has the limit raised to 100 (of course) and though we are yet to hit this limit we do regularly operate with 50–60 avatars on the dance-floor. At these times our region frame-rate suffers horribly, people crash (then return to hoorahs) and execution of scripts is delayed. But to be frank we don't really care, most members are used to it and it's wonderful to be in a vibrant venue whatever the impact on performance. We adjust our preferences, remain stationary, yell and enjoy the atmos'.

10 real-world brands

In this chapter you will learn:

- the value Second Life offers to real-world business
- about the opportunities available to real-world businesses
- how to approach positioning your business in-world

Real-world brands in Second Life

Second Life promises a whole new world of opportunities for an existing business or brand. Research firm Gartner Inc. estimates that by 2011, 80 per cent of active Internet users will have an identity in a virtual world and a recent Forrester report predicted that within five years, such platforms will become as significant a business tool as websites are today.

Communications, brand awareness, marketing and retail have historically been at the forefront of corporate Internet activity and it didn't take long for real-life businesses to exploit these existing benefits, then develop further opportunities on the thriving social networking environment that is the Second Life platform. Real-world businesses find in-world success in marketing and building brand awareness by advertising, hosting in-world events and offering experiences and inducements to generate the interest of residents. The 3D environment combined with real-time voice and text communication provides businesses with almost limitless opportunities for product testing, product feedback, business model analysis, market research, recruitment, training and maybe most exciting, real-time collaboration on projects.

Real-world businesses also find great value in Second Life by using their presence to enhance their productivity by reducing their employees' travelling time as well as cutting travel and accommodation costs by using Second Life for in-house training, meetings and events. Some find their value from the fact that prototypes can be quickly and inexpensively created using the Second Life viewer's built-in building tools. Others use the platform as a point of contact with the public and their customers for recruiting, exploring innovative retail techniques and market research.

None of the major companies or organizations establishing a presence in Second Life are currently looking at in-world profit as their primary motivation but instead are using Second Life as a way of developing their brand's reach and loyalty. They calculate that much like at the outset of the Internet phenomenon, it will be the most forward-looking companies that will reap the highest returns when everyone has an avatar. Against cost, the potential upside in global market reach is quite staggering.

Another significant attraction of the Second Life platform to real-world business is the relatively low start-up and operating costs. Second Life does not require any significant additional technology infrastructure.

Cisco seem to operate a excellent example and have over 1,000 employees active in-world. Cisco create value by owning restricted regions where they host both group level meetings and meetings of their international employees. Cisco also own several public regions where residents can train on Cisco products, where they receive customer feedback and display presentations using PowerPoint, video and streaming audio.

'We're definitely committed to Second Life,' Cisco's Jeanette Gibson told Reuters at the Virtual Worlds Conference in New York. 'Second Life is here to stay and so are we!'

Examining the opportunities

Marketing and brand awareness

There are currently (according to Linden Lab) a million active and individual long-term residents in the Second Life world with over a quarter of a million of us logging in every day. The fact of the matter is that wherever that volume of consumers congregate the marketers will seize the opportunity to build their brands.

As a result, companies have found value hosting events or offering in-world experiences or products to generate the interest of Second Life residents. For example, ING Renault F1 constructed a public racing track with very zippy karts to race around in. They have a very stylish workshop where I designed and fitted my racing helmet and an office offering information about the team and their sponsors, and I got to keep the kart!

I have toured many of the regions owned by the best known real-world brands currently operating in Second Life and though I have been impressed by some (though not nearly all) of their ideas, features, design and build quality I have been almost universally disappointed by the lack of resident activity at these venues. Brands certainly need to raise the bar when it comes to engaging residents by dedicating human resources to interact

ING Renault's F1 track – that's me at the wheel!

with their potential customers. Regular, fresh, innovative features and events need to be offered to instil value for both the brand asset and its visitors. Even when a Formula 1 team builds something this cool, the venue alone cannot hope to generate its own momentum.

Do not be lazy with your brand in Second Life. Do not be tempted into making the mistake of filling your region with camping stations. Becoming a camping parcel fools nobody into thinking a venue is either worth visiting or successful. The reality is that without erecting any resident attraction at all, any business can shoot to the top of the Second Life 'Popular Places' if the owners are prepared to pay campers enough. But camping provides neither a viable business model nor a good model for a community. Just like the rest of the Second Life community, the real-world brands that successfully locate here will be those brands that invest the most time and realize the most original ideas.

Recruitment

Of course brands that locate into Second Life are often best served by a core development team employed from within Second Life and this provides employment opportunities for both real- and in-world recruitment. Instead of posting a résumé, then attending a real-world interview, some residents are now being interviewed and hired for jobs. Linden Lab is a functioning example of this novel recruitment drive and offer a range of in-world and real-world jobs to residents who have had significant experience in Second Life. Successful candidates often don't have a background in professional content development or possess the real-world experiences usually required for such positions, but they have taken the time to become experts in Second Life.

Concept work, prototyping and simulating

The Second Life platform and the viewer's flexible building and scripting tools combine to create a near-perfect design and production tool for cost-effective, early-stage and rough 3D prototyping. The ability to brainstorm, assess, then evolve concept designs in real-time and earlier than has been previously possible, creates great value for those businesses utilizing the platform in this way.

For example, clothing manufacturers can develop their latest designs and ranges then apply the designs to a 3D human form without cutting a square inch of cloth. Vehicle manufacturers can create virtual prototypes, examine them and then adjust the thinking about various design decisions before reaching real-world prototype development.

The environment also provides an extraordinarily cost-effective method of simulating the real world for assessment purposes. For example, Swiss construction giant Implenia worked with IBM to investigate the most efficient ways to manage corporate lighting, by using virtual examples in their virtual buildings in Second Life, and the University of Maryland simulated a serious traffic accident to assess how well the emergency services responded. Innovative real-world real estate agents create virtual representations of the properties they have listed, allowing prospective buyers to visit and explore these properties.

Market research

Second Life features such as spatial voice and targeted group messaging allows brands to maintain a dialogue with residents.

A number of brands are engaging consumers via Second Life by forming focus groups around their brands, products and services and are using the platform as an effective method of conducting market research and receiving feedback from consumers around the world. Goodwill and product interest is fostered with customers and brand partners by introducing the latest real-world ideas in-world then distributing an equivalent virtual product in Second Life for cost-effective market assessment purposes and at the same time to develop brand loyalty.

Collaboration

The Second Life grid enables co-workers from different locations to collaborate on projects in real time by discussing and making decisions with their co-workers in a dynamic interactive 3D space. Groups of employees can cooperatively design then build their ideas and as the project evolves all those involved will be able to see the changes as they happen. Colleagues can walk around or through their projects to examine them from all angles and to thrash out the details, features and any improvements. Redgold and I working together to create the turntable in Chapter 7 is an entry-level example of this style of remote collaboration.

Collaborating on online projects using the Second Life platform allows businesses to offer a sense of presence and engagement to otherwise remote co-workers. A Second Life presence also encourages employee connections not possible in the real world. It is practically impossible for staff to meet randomly and strike up friendships using email and the telephone but the finance officer from Tokyo may notice the interesting human resources trainee from New York if they both happen to be wandering along the same virtual corridor at their organization's Second Life headquarters. They may strike up a conversation or invite each other to see what they have built or where they live. Much like culture in the real-world workplace the organization's sense of Second Life community inevitably evolves. Employees' avatars will also display a certain and I'm sure often remarkable, virtual expression of their characters not possible when using traditional Internet communication techniques.

Conducting meetings at virtual headquarters, creating employee only islands and office space, encouraging staff to meet in virtual entertainment and relaxation areas, throwing parties and holding events for far-flung employees; remote employee collaboration has never been cheaper, simpler or more immersive than when managed virtually from within Second Life.

Training

Traditional methods of training staff over the Internet have involved employees reading text documents, viewing slides and digesting videos. This model will be transformed as companies develop techniques using Second Life to train process and other workers in the same way as the US Marines use virtual reality to train troops. The platform provides organizations with the opportunity to employ more innovative ways to train employees and to host collaborative team-building exercises. The grid is a highly immersive and adaptable experience that can be used to simulate either the feel of a classroom or to create bespoke environments in which to simulate training exercises without the cost, risk and challenges of their real-world counterparts. Sales and marketing staff can also use the platform to practise and develop their presentations by having them assessed by their in-world colleagues.

Integrated communication solutions

Companies using Second Life to communicate are benefiting over users of traditional communication methods such as email, conference calls and travel. Second Life's 3-D spatial voice chat, multiple communication channels, open chat, instant messages and group notices are all provided as default features in the viewer which also supports multiple languages, character sets and keyboards. Second Life also provides useful communication tools such as the ability to stream live or pre-recorded audio and video, the upload and display of digital images and both can display and provide links to the wider Internet. As such the Second Life platform provides business with a cutting edge smorgasbord of real-time international and integrated communication solutions.

Retail

The functionality currently available from the Linden Scripting Language does not yet support e-commerce web services such as a shopping cart. In the meantime in-world retail of real world products is managed using web-links. For example we act as both Amazon and iTunes affiliates and are currently piloting in-world both a bookstore and a record store where residents can browse the titles selected to be in keeping with our themes then click on a vendor which will direct the customer's system to the relevant web site.

Retailing real world products in a virtual world

I see significant potential for real-world product retailing in Second Life as virtual malls provide a low-cost platform that permits multiple buyers to browse and interact in real time within a retailer's purpose-built 3D space.

The real excitement lies when Internet users develop the same confidence in browsing for and purchasing real-world goods and services in-world as we currently feel when shopping online using traditional websites. Again I believe the brands that will stand out in Second Life will be those businesses that dedicate human resources to their virtual asset. Businesses should no more consider opening an unstaffed Second Life retail outlet than they would entertain the notion of launching an unstaffed real-world location.

Customer service

Businesses using the Second Life platform can provide a far superior point of contact for their customers than the traditional call-centre model. Otherwise difficult conversations with disgruntled customers can be conducted one-on-one, in private and within comfortable surroundings. Any periods that require the customer to be 'put on hold' no longer create frustration for our client, but can be used to entertain, educate or otherwise stimulate or even relax our troubled resident.

'Miss Tsure, I'm very sorry to hear you have been so upset by the difficulty you are experiencing installing our product. I will IM a member of our technical team who will TP you to the workshop and using a virtual demonstration will take you through the entire installation process. While we set that up and to calm you down, I would like to invite you to step into our crystal meditation room for a scalp massage.'

I foresee an entirely new virtual customer services workforce that will emerge from those Second Life residents who are disabled, mothers with young children and the elderly. These and a whole host of other residents who require a more flexible and home-based style of occupation can be incorporated within a virtual customer services workforce and yet a sense of connection to both the workplace and colleagues can be maintained in a way not possible using the traditional, uninspiring and lonely home-worker model.

Custom Second Life last names

Linden Lab offer custom last names to organizations in order that a business's employees may share a common Second Life identity. Custom last names must be organizational in construction to be easily distinguishable from personal last names. For example 'Irie' would not be acceptable to Linden Lab as a custom last name, but 'IrieEnterprises' probably would be. Custom names cost US$1,000 to set up and then US$500 annually.

Employing experts

Throughout every other chapter in this book I urge Second Life residents not to employ experts but instead to learn the required skills themselves. Obviously this strategy may not be practical to apply when a real-world business or brand wishes to create their Second Life presence.

If your business has limited in-house experience of virtual worlds then it is certainly worth considering employing a developer or team of developers from within the Second Life community to advise you on land purchase, design, build and most crucially, content and features. Be wary of hiring PR applicants or professional computer programmers from the real world, as these may have little understanding or experience in the idiosyncrasies of conducting business virtually.

A real-life professional (an architect for example) brings a lot less relevant expertise to Second Life than a resident experienced in working within its unique environment. Many of the rules and techniques that apply to real life just do not apply in-world. Many problems exist in Second Life that require solutions, strategies and thinking not adopted elsewhere. For example, most residents' viewer draw distance is limited to 64–128m. Designs need to accommodate this relevant detail amongst many other unique design challenges such as sense of space, lag and the fact that residents can teleport and even fly!

People who have been creating content in Second Life for years might not be considered professional content developers elsewhere, but we are used to such quirks and therefore have become the real experts in this unique and new environment. Within Second Life (and for the time being) we are the best there is.

When you think you have found a suitable candidate from the pool of Second Life experience, spend some time examining their existing work within Second Life and talking with their clients.

Staffing virtual assets

Understanding that real employees are required to staff virtual assets is a current business blind-spot it seems to me. As we have discussed over and over again, simply building something has never been enough to maintain mainstream resident interest. Let us not forget that a deserted attraction communicates just as clearly a brand's level of innovation and commitment to its customers as does a ram-packed and popular venue.

marketing in second life

In this chapter you will learn:

- how to use a group to promote your enterprise
- how to post classifieds and events
- about other marketing opportunities

Whatever your business, to thrive, word of your existence will need to spread. Marketing in Second Life takes many forms and here we examine the most common marketing strategies and techniques applied in Second Life in the order of usefulness as I have found them.

Branding

Create a specific brand name and logo for your in-world business in order that residents learn to immediately recognize your efforts. Take the time to identify the brand with shapes, colour combinations, fonts and words that please the eye and identify with your target markets. I create our logos using MS Office products but you will also find free web-based logo creation services using your preferred search engine.

Second Life groups

Whatever your business model entails, the Second Life group system will be a key tool to assist your Second Life marketing. Residents create groups in order to bind a community together but we use the group as a customer database from which to communicate and market. The Irie Vibes group currently boasts over 6,000 members of which the majority are active accounts (i.e. have logged on over the last couple of months). This means that we can communicate directly with thousands of potential customers as often as we like, at any given time and for any reason. This is a very powerful marketing tool that we use to great success with both business and social applications.

- Creating a Second Life group costs L$100.

- A group that has fewer than two members for any 48-hour period will be automatically deleted. Register an alt (alternative account) for yourself and join it to the group to avoid this happening.

To create a Second Life group:

1 Select **Edit > Groups** from the viewer's top menu bar to display the **Groups** tab of the **Communicate** window.

2 Click the **Create...** button to display the **Group Information** template into which we enter our new group's details.

3 Under the **General** tab enter the name of the group.

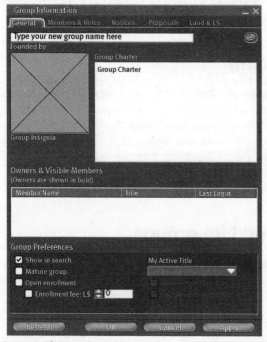

4 The **Group Charter** panel is used to describe our group.

5 A logo or texture can be dragged from the inventory onto the **Group Insignia** panel to be displayed in the group's profile.

6 Tick the **Show in search** checkbox unless the group is intended to be private.

7 Tick the **Mature group** checkbox if the group will be conducting adult-orientated activities.

8 Choose whether to enable **Open enrollment** so that residents can join the group without an invitation.

9 Elect whether to charge an **Enrollment fee** to join your group, and if so then how much.

10 Clicking the **OK** button will create the group and L$100 will be taken from your Second Life account.

To invite someone to join your Second Life group, you right-click on their avatar then select **More > Group Invite** from the pie menu. The **Groups** window opens listing groups to which we have permission to invite other residents. Select the relevant group then click the **OK** button.

Group roles

Group members can be assigned to specific roles within the group and each group role issued with a defining (or amusing) group title. A group is initially created containing three roles but we may define up to ten roles. The three default roles are:

- **Owners:** Group owners control and have access to all group abilities. The Owners role cannot be deleted or renamed.

- **Officers:** Officers control and have access to many but not all group abilities. The role may be deleted or renamed.

- **Everyone:** This default role contains everyone in the group and defines the basic abilities for all members of the group. The Everyone role cannot be deleted or renamed.

This image illustrates three distinct roles within a single Second Life group. Members assigned these different roles have been granted different group abilities, for example the DJ role has the

ability to change the group land media URLs, the host role comes with the ability to join new members and send group notices whilst the VIP role is the default 'everyone' role.

From the **Members & Roles** tab of the Group Information window we find three further sub-tabs:

- **Members:** From the Members sub-tab we invite and eject members from the group.

- **Roles:** From the Roles sub-tab we create and edit group roles and also grant abilities to group roles.

  To create a role we click the **Create New Role...** button, rename the role, decide on the title (group tag) then carefully assign abilities to the new role from the Allowed Abilities panel.

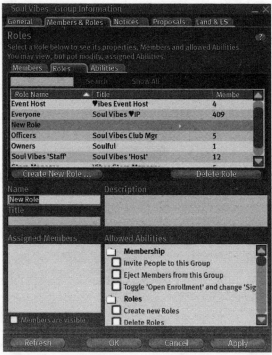

- **Abilities:** From the Abilities sub-tab we can identify those roles and members possessing each ability and view descriptions of all group abilities.

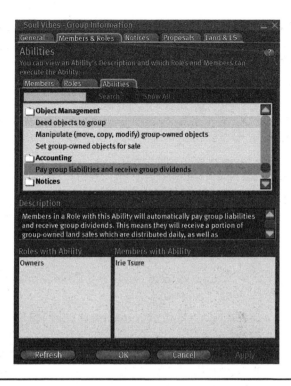

Irie note

It is most important to ensure that you have selected only appropriate roles to accounting responsibilities. Group members will not be impressed if they discover that they are unwittingly contributing to the group's liabilities.

Group notices

Sending group notices offers an extremely effective method to keep in touch with the group and comes with the option to attach an item. When a group notice is sent, a pop-up message is delivered to all group members and therefore notices may be used for all manner of marketing purposes such as announcing events, sales, or new products and delivering freebies, landmarks and flyers (as textures).

Notices can only be sent by group members in roles granted the ability to send notices and are only received by group members in roles granted the ability to receive notices.

Promoting your business

Appearing in the Second Life search results

It is vital to success to ensure that the business is listed within Second Life search results:

1 Right-click directly on the parcel's ground then select **About Land** from the pie menu.

2 From the **Options** tab of the About Land window tick the Show Place in Search (L$30/week) checkbox.

3 Select a category from the drop-down menu that best defines your business.

4 Tick the Mature Content checkbox if your business is adult-orientated.

Placing classifieds in Second Life

It often proves profitable for Second Life businesses to place classified advertisements in order to be visible alongside relevant search results. Classifieds are sorted by the amount residents pay, with the highest fees being displayed first. We place classified advertisements from our Second Life Profile and from within the parcel where our visitor attraction is based:

1 Access your profile then select the **Classified** tab.

2 Click the **New** button.

3 Enter the name and a description then set the location.

4 A logo or prepared texture can be dragged from the inventory onto the image panel.

5 Select a category from the drop-down menu that best defines your business.

6 Tick the **Mature Content** checkbox if appropriate.

7 Tick the 'Auto-renew each week' checkbox if you wish the advertisement to be automatically placed each week. For the duration of your advertisement's placement your Second Life account will be automatically billed each week at the set price. Leaving this checkbox un-ticked will result in the advertisement being withdrawn at the conclusion of the currently booked week.

8 Clicking the Publish button displays the window into which we enter then set the weekly price we want to pay for our advertisement.

Click-thru statistics

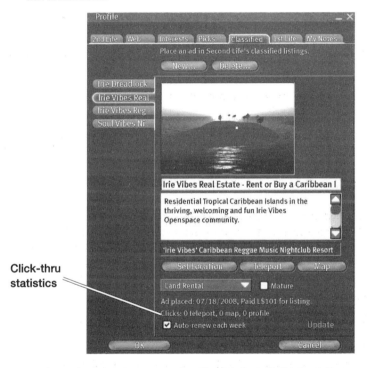

Apart from the price, we can edit all of a classified ad's information after publication and then save any changes by clicking the **Update** or **OK** button.

Click-thru statistics are displayed within our own classified advertisements. These statistics are not visible to other residents and are there to help us assess the effectiveness of our classifieds.

Post your Second Life events

Whether you are a venue operator or retailer, hosting and posting events is an effective method of attracting customers. Examples of Second Life events include discussions, meetings, live music, DJs and dances, classes, tours and competitions. Second Life residents may post up to five events per day (including event edits) from the **Community: Events** page of the Second Life website. Events that we post appear both on the website and under the Events tab of viewer's Search window ([**Ctrl**] + [**F**]).

Other useful Second Life marketing strategies

◆ Encourage your satisfied customers to list your business or service under their Profile 'Picks' tab. Residents read the profiles of other residents and being a 'Pick' also contributes to raising a business in the Second Life search results.

◆ Providing free items is a tried and tested method of encouraging residents to your location.

◆ Forward your innovative and high quality products with details of your business to the editors of Second Life related blogs and magazines.

◆ Add any relevant services you provide to the Solution Providers section of the Second Life website. Solution Providers are considered individuals or businesses that hire out their services to create content for Second Life.

◆ Build and maintain a traditional website.

appendices

A: Irie's summary of success

Adapt and Evolve

Second Life enterprise is still in its infancy and as such I fiercely believe that most opportunities still lie ahead of us. There is little solid reference material available that residents can refer to in order to research which of our ideas might flourish and which may flounder. It therefore becomes important to experiment, evolve and adapt in the attempt to identify winning formulae.

Have no fear and hold no embarrassment of failure when experimenting with business models. Some ideas work and some don't and there is usually only one way to find out. Some of my most exciting ideas have fizzled away into nothingness. On the other hand the venue of Irie Vibes was an after-thought to three homes I erected to rent out. Irie Vibes has gone on to become a Second Life highlight, a defining music venue and in my (not so humble) opinion, the most vibrant and positive community in Second Life. But a nightclub was not in my original thinking and its rapid evolution took me by surprise.

The key to the success of Irie Vibes was my willingness to quickly abandon my original concept and concentrate upon what was patently working. I did not rigidly inflict my predefined plan on residents but rather allowed the market to define our position and ultimately to form a highly successful business model.

If you regularly visit our regions you are still likely to encounter rapid change as I continue to experiment with new features, designs and strategies in order to identify further opportunities. This process maintains a freshness in our venues and also develops my own skills, techniques and strategies.

Start small

Ironically, just before I sat down to commence this chapter an old friend IMed me to ask me to come and cast my eye over his latest venture. This friend (who shall remain nameless) has opened at least four clubs over the last year and unfortunately all have closed within a few months of their launch.

A prefabricated 4-storey castle rezzed in front of me! The structure was huge and erected on a quarter sim of Mainland purchased specifically for the project. My friend loves castles and big ones at that. But such passions cost money and the income this monster will need to generate to cover his investment and ongoing costs will not be insignificant. If the club does not provide income quickly, the money my friend makes as a Land Baron will again be eaten away. I think he may struggle.

If I was in my friend's position, I would rent a couple of thousand square metres maximum. My only cost would be this land. Growing the venue would take time, but time I hope I have. I would carefully craft the small and intimate castle of my dreams and within my castle I would create a cosy little club, probably somewhat brighter than the rest of the castle to invite contrast and focus to the build. I would create somewhere I loved to be and then invite my friends over. And that would be the beginning of it. Invest time into your ideas; not money.

Watch the market

Keep your business eyes open for opportunities to plug any gaps in the market. For example, within the first few months of opening our reggae venue, we had attracted three retailers of dreadlock-style hair products. The resident Booperfunk did very well, expanded then moved onto her own sim. The two other retailers disappeared. For a few weeks I was regularly asked by visitors where dreadlocks could be purchased. Eventually when no dreadlock retailers arrived I created a small range to fill the gap. I made less than a dozen styles and have never added to the range, yet selling dreadlocks has provided a consistent additional income of over L$30,000 per month. I have the right products in a well-positioned store on a popular sim. More importantly I keep my eyes open for opportunities. During that period the hundreds of other residents passing through were presented with precisely the same opportunity. At that time anyone deciding to learn to make dreadlocks, producing and maintaining a comprehensive range and opening the store would have made an awful lot more money than I did. I have only ever had time to dip a metaphoric toe into retail.

Learn everything

Never spend money on something you can learn to do yourself. Take the time to learn to be a proficient builder and scripter. Whatever your primary business focus, these skills will permit you to create content precisely as you want to and provide firm foundations for your future as a Second Life entrepreneur.

Spending days or weeks learning and practising a skill will accelerate your success as you will be able to provide your own solutions and designs to fill your needs. These solutions and designs provide additional products and services you can retail to other Second Life residents and business owners.

Employ great staff

Hiring good staff is essential for growth, for as a business develops it becomes impossible to handle all the roles personally. Your staff will act as your personal and the business's representatives and it is therefore crucial that you consider prospective staff very carefully. Hire your staff from your regular customers. They are already supporting the venture by being there and in my experience, are delighted to support the community further.

Most staff will drift away eventually so always be on the lookout for enthusiastic and appropriate members who may be interested in supporting the community further by acting as staff members.

Managing growth and expectations

Don't expect instant success and don't give up the day job! Working consistently to produce quality items and to offer services of value is the way to get ahead in Second Life. But the process takes a little time.

Grow only as the business can afford to do so. I bought our first sim only when the income to purchase and maintain it was already being generated. I bought our second sim only when the first sim was generating the necessary income to purchase and maintain the second. I keep our overheads comfortably within income boundaries and this allows us to operate without time restraint or financial pressures. It also allows me to experiment freely and to make my mistakes without threatening the stability of the underlying business model. Of course we could have stayed at one sim and this would have produced a tidy and stable monthly profit but I have grander plans.

Accounting

Each Linden dollar transaction (including L$0 transactions) is uniquely numbered. Details of all your transactions during the last 30 days are accessed by clicking the Transactions History link found on the My Account page of the Second Life website. More extensive lists of your transactions can also be downloaded as XML files from this web page. As business operators we should use this data to stay aware of our income and outgoings, to keep an eye on which of our projects is generating the most cash-flow and to identify any significant or unexpected sinks.

The Account History link on the same page will lead you to the US$ billing history for your account. Details such as your currency exchange orders (i.e. either buying or selling Linden dollars using the LindeX) are shown here as well as Linden tier and land purchase fees.

European Union residents are required to pay VAT (17.5–20%) on all services they buy from Linden Lab (e.g. LindeX transaction fees, Mainland/region purchases, tier, etc.) and therefore if we do not register for VAT we are at a considerable financial disadvantage to entrepreneurial residents living outside the EU. It is therefore prudent to look into voluntarily registering for a VAT number at the first sign of not-insignificant land bills. As a UK resident, registering my valid VAT number with Linden Lab in effect reduces my estate tier payments by 17.5% and places me back on a level playing field with the rest of the world.

A word on business partnerships

The overwhelming majority of successful Second Life businesses, that I have noticed, are solo ventures. This certainly does not preclude successful partnerships and I am aware of several amazingly productive business partnerships, but more often than not these arrangements quickly end in tears.

I have been tempted towards a business partner myself on a few occasions, usually when things aren't going so well or I am just inundated with too many tasks, but I have resisted for three main reasons:

1 Without reference to anyone I can change anything or everything. I have total creative and inspirational freedom. I could not work so well or so fast if I needed to discuss or justify my thinking.

2 Divide my income?! I would need to understand just how a partner would at least double my potential for any partnership to be worth considering. If Second Life does develop into a vast Internet phenomenon then I am well positioned to benefit and would be frustrated to feel I had given a large slice of the potential reward away just to have my hand held.

3 I cannot be abandoned. The woe I have witnessed when one partner decides that they have had enough. I know that I can rely on myself!

Up to now I have been prepared to take the time to learn whatever skills I felt a prospective partner could bring to my operations. This principle of self-reliance has provided the basis to my Second Life entrepreneurial adventure.

B: My past, our present and the future

I arrived in Second Life without the vaguest idea of how anything worked, why I was there and what I would do. A little of my time was my initial investment. Learning to create and sell a few little objects then allowed me to develop the skills to generate an entrepreneurial spark.

My path led me to explore the business landscape by dabbling in real-estate, manufacture, retail and venue management. I am now a 'jack of all trades' but remain a master of none. This is where I want to be. My first joy has been in the learning process, my second in the community that was accidently born.

Had my wish been to maximize profit taking (and there is absolutely no shame in that ambition!!) I would have specialized in one sector, and most probably retailing hair. My dreadlocks have sold consistently well for over a year and if I had made a few new products each week since I would probably need a sim just to sell the range. I imagine my income would be significantly greater than it currently is. But that was never my interest.

I am a social entrepreneur. I feel my role is to oversee our thriving community. Managing the needs of the social group itself now takes as much time as managing the business. Residents have problems, issues and triumphs to discuss. Conflicts need resolving.

As such we are profit making but not profit taking. Our income gets ploughed back into funding the community and our profit put towards improving our members' experience and growth. So it remains important that the business makes good money and is managed well.

My future

Over the last six months or so, one of my Second Life projects has been writing this book of course and I hope its contribution will be that the early learning of content creation skills becomes seen as an automatic part of the experience. As more residents create content and form successful enterprises then the environment will become richer for all residents.

Like you, I still feel that I am at the outset of my journey through Second Life. As I write I've still not yet been in-world for two years. I've just touched the canvas but most of my ideas I believe are yet to come, as I hope is most of my creativity and progress. Irie Vibes as a community will continue to command my primary focus as it is this arena in which I feel I can do the most worthwhile work and therefore reap the most satisfaction.

As my 'to do' list keeps growing, I know my future will be in at least the short to medium term, pretty hectic. I remain excited and optimistic about the future of Irie Tsure. She has energy, works hard and works smart. She is surrounded by creative people and with lots of love and support.

Irie's 'To Do' List (in no particular order)

1   Extend my clothing and hair product ranges.

2   Develop retail versions of the unique or improved products and scripts that I have designed initially for our use, e.g. our DJ tip ball, turntables, staff HUDs, etc.

3   Open further nightclubs and regions focused around other musical genres using the successful Irie Vibes business model, e.g. Soul Vibes, Urban Vibes, Latin Vibes, Jazz Vibes, etc.

4   Extend the Irie Real Estate business as a resident of good reputation.

5   Further explore retailing real-world products in Second Life using affiliate programs and web-links provided by brands such as iTunes and Amazon.

6   Explore retailing real-world Irie Vibes branded merchandising such as Irie Vibes mugs and T-shirts.

7   Develop the in-world Irie Vibes newspaper.

8   Create an Irie Vibes Internet radio station.

9   Write Irie Tsure's autobiography (and perhaps a novel based within Second Life).

10 Make a Machinima movie.

11 Become Chief Advisor to the CEO of Linden Lab.

As my journey progresses I hope that Irie Vibes continues its march towards becoming an important global community promoting the values that I hold to be important. Of course I also trust that I will continue to identify more opportunities to add to my 'to do' list. Sometimes I feel we are experiencing an atmosphere similar to the discovery of fire or the development of the personal computer... we are devising loads of applications for our finding and the pace of this invention is rapid.

The future of Second Life

The lag many residents currently deal with will become a thing of the past as computer processing becomes both cheaper and more powerful and as the Second Life platform evolves. If you remember dial-up Internet connections you will know exactly the process I'm referring to.

Despite predictable brouhaha and scepticism from the usual suspects, it seems quite likely that Second Life shows us the future structure of Internet activity. Our virtual world offers its residents both a simpler and more comprehensible model than the traditional Internet experience in so much as homepages appear to us in-world as the familiar 3D homes and business headquarters that we are accustomed to, image slide-shows are presented as art galleries, e-commerce is represented by shops and stores and Internet chat-rooms now place us on a dance floor then immerse us in flashing lights and loud music. Most significantly we see and can interact with the other Internet users.

In essence, Second Life resembles our real-world understanding so closely that it offers a far more natural experience for Internet users than when web-browsing. Second Life links the Internet to our real-world experiences by tapping into the familiar and comfortable spatial and memory techniques that humans have evolved over the millennia to exist in our real world. The inevitable result manifests both in resident hours increasing (because it is more stimulating here than the wider Internet) and in more and more applications transferring from the traditional Internet into Second Life.

The open source project will create added functionality such as portals through which residents will pass into other virtual worlds. Our websites, phones and TV will all become accessible in-world and offer seamless functionality.

I find it impossible to imagine hundreds of thousands and maybe millions of residents simultaneously wandering the grid, but I do remember when Bill launched MS Windows 95 and explained to us how we'd all have PCs in our homes, how we'd communicate by sending e-messages and how we would shop and pay bills using business 'web-sites'. Oh how we scoffed!

We can only guess the shape of future virtual worlds, but what I am certain of, and in spite our most optimistic and fantastic imaginings, is that in just a few years we will be sitting down and saying to each other 'I thought the future might be impressive, but never in a million years would I have guessed it would be like this!' and I intend to be fully involved in this revolution.

Good luck in all that you do, see you in-world and thank you for listening.

Grie Tsure Xxx

C: Useful keyboard shortcuts

User Interface

[F1]	Help
[Home]	Fly
[M]	Mouselook
[Esc]	Reset to default view
[Ctrl] + [F]	Search window
[Ctrl] + [G]	Active gestures
[Ctrl] + [H]	Chat history window
[Ctrl] + [I]	Inventory
[Ctrl] + [M]	World map
[Ctrl] + [Shift] + [M]	Mini-map
[Ctrl] + [P]	Preferences window
[Ctrl] + [R]	Always run
[Ctrl] + [U]	Upload image
[Ctrl] + [T]	Communicate window
[Ctrl] + [Shift] + [S]	Snapshot
[Ctrl] + [Shift] + [']	Snapshot to disk
[Ctrl] + [Shift] + [A]	Start/Stop video to disk
[Ctrl] + [Shift] + [W]	Close all windows
[Ctrl] + [Alt] + [1]	Show/hide user interface (i.e. windows, menus etc.)
[Ctrl] + [Shift] + [1]	Show/hide Statistics window
[Ctrl] + [Alt] + [Shift] + [P]	Show/hide land parcel boundaries

Menus

[Ctrl] + [1]	Focus menu
[Ctrl] + [2]	Move menu
[Ctrl] + [3]	Edit menu

| [Ctrl] + [4] | Create menu |
| [Ctrl] + [5] | Land menu |

Editing

[G]	Snap selected object to the building grid
[H]	Focus viewer to selected object
[Ctrl] + [L]	Link selected objects
[Ctrl] + [Shift] + [L]	Unlink selected objects
[Ctrl] + [Z]	Undo
[Ctrl] + [Y]	Redo

Advanced menu

[Ctrl] + [Alt] + [D]	Show/hide Advanced menu
[Ctrl] + [Alt] + [T]	Toggle Highlight Transparent
[Ctrl] + [Alt] + [R]	Rebake textures

index